WITH GUN & GOWN

THE AUTOBIOGRAPHY OF A SOLDIER & SCHOLAR

NORMAN FRISKNEY

WITH GUN & GOWN

THE AUTOBIOGRAPHY OF A SOLDIER & SCHOLAR

MEMOIRS

Cirencester

Published by Memoirs

MEMOIRS
PUBLISHING

25 Market Place, Cirencester, Gloucestershire, GL7 2NX
info@memoirsbooks.co.uk www.memoirspublishing.com

First published in England, June 2013

Book jacket design Ray Lipscombe

ISBN 978-1-86151-009-9

Printed in England

CONTENTS

Foreword
Introduction

1   The troopship   Page 1

2   Infantry reinforcements   Page 19

3   Into battle   Page 29

4   Transit camps and troop trains   Page 39

5   On leave with the Allies   Page 52

6   The black market   Page 60

7   Taking stock   Page 72

8   The aftermath of war   Page 78

9   A village childhood   Page 87

10 Grammar school days   Page 110

11 Oxford, moribund   Page 121

12 Gelded youth   Page 128

13 Headhunting and other sports   Page 137

14 Pupils, parents and pranks   Page 154

15 Staying a head   Page 167

16 Out of the classroom   Page 177

17 Full circle   Page 186

FOREWORD

That which follows is only in part autobiographical and is in substantial part anecdotal. The later chapters relate to village life in the 1930s; much of it is in light vein and I hope anecdotally amusing. There follows some interesting material about Oxford University in both the pre-war and later post-war period, when amongst others I was to meet the King of Bechuanaland, Harold Wilson, Anton Walbrook (the film actor), Edmund Blunden and others less well known, all of whom provide a background to stories worth recounting.

The period of the war relates the experiences of a young infantry officer, and apart from front-line battle descriptions tells something of wartime military hospitals, encounters with the military mafia, first meetings with the Russians flown in from Yugoslavia, a meeting with Kesselring's girlfriend and the accidental breaking of Mussolini's bed by myself and a friend. This section is mainly culled from my own war diaries, and although lodged in the archives of the Imperial War Museum is unpublished. I retain the copyright.

There follow chapters about changes in education in the post-war period, written in the form of anecdotes and encounters with a wide spectrum of well known people such as Margaret Thatcher, Roy Hattersley, Sir William Penney (who oversaw Britain's nuclear bomb), the Reverend John

Nicholls (Chaplain to the Queen), Bernard Weatherill (the former Speaker), and many others. This material is hitherto also unpublished. Much of the fabric of this part of the work is interwoven with humorous stories relating to 25 years of grammar school headmastering and of other well-known heads of school in London and elsewhere. Stories such as the use of a grammar school headmistress's house as a brothel have not previously been recounted in print.

The latter part of the book is linked with some of the earlier material and contains a certain amount of light verse. Whilst directly relevant to the work (and my own writing), it was published last year in a journal at Oxford University, but it has had only limited circulation.

NJF

INTRODUCTION

One of the fascinations of any visit to the National Gallery, even if, like myself, you claim to be but a disciple rather than a discerning member of the cognoscenti of the fine arts, derives from looking at landscapes, townscapes or seascapes of past centuries, created long before photography became the commonplace visual interpretation of today. Dress, costume, carriages, roads, cornfields and reapers, ships and boats, all the still-life artefacts of man, the interiors of dwellings, the bygones of the past seen in the context of living rather than in the museum, bring to vivid life a world we have lost. So whilst the landscapes of mountains and the seascapes and sunsets remain unchanging, I look with more interest upon the imprint of the past that man has placed upon them.

Alternatively, a stimulus to the senses which is evocative of yesteryear is equally, or better, awakened through great writings, be it the London of Pepys or Dickens, the Wessex of Hardy, the China of Marco Polo or any of the countless vivid canvasses painted by those who put pen to paper in their day and age. These come to us first hand. They have an advantage over the researcher, the historical novelist or today's descriptive wordsmiths of bygone scenes, for the only filters between their day and ours are their pens and our imaginations. Whether the vernacular be that of Caesar or Chaucer, it brings to life the past in dimensions that the contemporary writer of scenes long since gone must always struggle to reproduce.

We all possess in memory a world of the past we have inhabited, and with age that world, although receding, becomes more and more rapidly a lost one. Motorways, aircraft in the sky, destruction by developers and the machines that make all these things possible as the rate of technical progress snowballs have obscured or blotted out these canvasses with new paint, often into unrecognisability. Those of us who can recall these lost worlds, simpler times which still carried echoes of the years before 1914, remember often with nostalgia our lost landscapes. So may some others of later generations feel an echo of that nostalgia for a world that they themselves have not known at first hand.

I write therefore not out of an old man's sentimentality or an 'Oh that I were young again and she were in my arms', or, indeed, for a *recherche du temps perdu*, for like all fortunate golden lads and lasses I was lucky to become gilded before becoming metaphorically gelded. But to evoke these lost worlds, to reverse, as it were, the arrow of time in the imagination, the wordsmith must try to recreate more than the artefacts and activities of a past age. Somehow he must try to recapture the spirit, the personality of yesterday, what indeed it was like to be young in the years between the two great wars, or to march with the infantry in one of them. If, then, there is any measure of success to be had in writing of such things, it would be realised that if a reader born 25 or 50 years ago were able to say 'Yes, if I had been born in 1920 or 1940, that might have been the feel of life for me, the spirit of an age now past!'

We can all ask such questions at different levels, and even, with Larkin, reminisce on delectable things that began in 1960. It is trite to say it, but one journey we can never make and which might be the most exciting one of all would be to live in the mind of another person, even more so within the mind of one of the opposite sex, which we might truly find to be a foreign land. But writing can sometimes enable us to help provide a passport for the traveller to enter into, at least as a visitor, the strange world inhabited by another.

When I was an undergraduate I had much dialogue with my tutor at Oxford about the twin philosophical propositions of possibilism and determinism as affecting the life of man in history and geography on our planet. The doctrines, indeed, of the extent to which we control our destinies or the measure in which they are determined for us. When we are very young our lives are largely guided and controlled by outside agencies, and even as we grow older and think ourselves free we are to some extent everywhere in chains. But the choice of the possibilities does open rather wider for the more fortunate, be it through the power of the will to direct their own lives and to some degree, for good or ill, those of others. In retrospect and reflection, if we are lucky, an analysis of all this might seem to give to life a purpose and a meaning.

So in spite of some who might say there are lies, damned lies and autobiographies (and I hope you may not say *'s'excuser est s'accuser'*) and before the marinade of alcohol or the mists of age destroy or dim further the cerebral synapses, I will try to paint the canvas of a past age as well as I may and flesh out some of its bones. If I have any success in breathing into them the spirit of a time that has gone, it would indeed be enough if a few of my contemporaries were able to say with me, dear reader 'Yes, yes, that's how it was'. If I were able to paint the picture for those much younger than myself and some of them were able to say the same, that would be success indeed, for, as I shall seek to show, there are no generations, only people.

CHAPTER ONE

THE TROOPSHIP

Forgive me if I still trespass in your dreams
Nightmares shared once by light of common day
In war full seventy years ago, for yet it seems
That years between roll soft like mists away
When only night could bring the balm
And sleep could close its curtain on the day.

Forgive me if I still trespass in your dreams
Those shades and shadows of so long ago
Those drifting, insubstantial scenes
That only we as sole survivors know.
Forgive, for as in night's long hours confine
You in my dreams, can still enter mine.

NJF

It was 1941, and I was eighteen years of age. As I took my seat in hall at Jesus College, Oxford for the scholarship examinations, there was but one title for the first, an essay paper entitled 'The European Tradition'. During the three hours allowed I thought of my father in the war we still called

1

the Great War. His health undermined in years in Mesopotamia; others of our family in Flanders. The European Tradition. And so I wrote of the tragedy afflicted on our continent in its centuries of tribal conflicts. Not for me to recount the classical story of our Christian civilisation. War and sacrifice - that was the story we absorbed in those schooldays in the thirties. 'The sand of the desert is sodden red, red with the blood of a square that broke' And there's some corner of a foreign field that is forever England', and on Armistice Day how we were to bring 'no maimed or worthless sacrifice'. Brainwashed by Kipling, saddened by the war poets (I was soon to sit at the feet of one, Edmund Blunden, at Oxford). And so Antony and I wrote our essays. Antony, like me, was to be awarded an Exhibition and his personal number when we were commissioned was to be next to mine. Antony was as a brother, and he served with me until he was killed in battle just before it all ended. The likelihood as infantry subalterns is that one in three will survive one will be wounded and one will be not.

And so it was that I should be the lucky one to shoulder the guilt of survival and write of those times. *Dulce et decorum est pro patria mori* (Wilfred Owen) - it is a sweet and seemly thing to die for one's country.

I am an infantry man. We are marching out of Lime Street station on a cold, grey morning in Liverpool early in 1944 to embark at the docks and join our regiments at the front in Italy. The invasion of Western Europe is to happen in a few months' time. But we do not know that. Neither do we know where we are going. We speculate that it could be Burma. The only bridgehead we have in Europe is in southern Italy, and the great battle for Cassino is still raging. *Dulce et decorum est...*

There are shadows cast by the past over the lives of those

who live in the present. 1914-1918 - the trenches, Passchendaele, the Somme - and we have read the war poets: Siegfried Sassoon, Wilfred Owen, Edmund Blunden. Both Owen and Sassoon, in their generation men of strength and sensitivity, had for some time mended their shattered nerves at the Craiglochhart military hospital in Scotland, and as a cadet I had watched Edmund Blunden's face as he lectured undergraduates in the Senior Training Corps at Oxford in the year I had spent as an undergraduate before joining the 124th Officer Cadet Training Unit in Wales. I wondered how we would fare. The shadows that had seemed to move across Blunden's face were the same shadows that had lengthened as the sun set over the young lives lost in that last holocaust, the mud and blood of Flanders. And so we fought the battles that were inevitably to come, vicariously in our imaginations, in terms of the frightfulness of the last great conflict. Death and glory. *Dulce et decorum est.*

'Blunden's given up lecturing to the STC' they said in the Junior Common Room at Jesus College. 'He can't face for them what he knows they face themselves.' But so far it hadn't worked out that way. As we marched out of Lime Street Station past the Mersey Tunnel entrance, my thoughts turned to my first couple of years in the army after that initial year at Oxford; the University STC and 'Certificate B'. We had been the last of the blue-eyed boys. No other-rank service for us. Straight to an Officer Cadet Training Unit in Wales in our university blazers and scarves. The NCOs of the permanent staff had looked us over with scepticism as we detrained at Llandrindod Wells Station. 'Left, right, left, right. Pick 'em up gentlemen!' We looked a healthy lot. 'Battle school will sort' em out. ' Seven months of training in the Welsh mountains in winter.

Half the battery comprised young undergraduates from Oxford and Cambridge - and in the end we showed them how. We were into action with the guns more quickly than the old sweats. Oxford and Cambridge versus the rest, it had been. So many memories. 'Mad' Major Braithwaite on the Welsh Hills: 'Now, gentlemen, if you spray a group of men with a machine gun you are unlikely to hit any of them. Give me the Bren. See that flock of sheep on the other side of the valley?'

A quick turn on the heel and off went a magazine. It was an unsuccessful demonstration, resulting in compensation for a farmer and mutton in the officers' mess for dinner for a week. There was mountain training on motor cycles, evenings in the NAAFI with Frank Hauser of Christ Church at the piano, later to achieve fame at the Oxford Playhouse. Drinking with Officer-Cadet Bill Connor, aka Cassandra of the *Daily Mirror*, and listening to his stories of high people in high places. Gin and the Warsaw Concerto with Captain Houston Barnes, our troop commander. The naming of parts and the sheer dull misery of active minds learning and relearning the tedious trade of war. But this was all in the past. We had done our homework, and so we marched out into the Liverpool morning.

I know the city well, for I have spent most of the past year manning a 'Z' rocket battery on Bootle cycle stadium. But I am no longer a gunner. Over a thousand young officers like myself have spent the past two months in Dunbar learning the arts of infantry warfare. The Luftwaffe no longer threatens Liverpool. The enemy comes no more to us, so we must go to him.

It had been a strange interlude. The summer of 1943 had been hot and dry. Here in the centre of the cycle track at Bootle we had kicked our heels with our 64 rocket projectors and our ammunition shelters stocked with their racks of cordite-filled eight-foot drainpipes, each attached to a shell and a fuse. Set the fuse, pull the rocket on the rails, move the projector to the appointed spot, elevate the contraption, press a switch, and if you are lucky the current ignites the cordite and off she goes into the sky. As it leaves the projector it sounds like an express train passing through a station. Seconds later the pre-set fuse explodes the shell. There is a roll of thunder, but rarely does it seem to do any damage to the enemy. The remains of the contraption - the drainpipe in which the cordite charge is contained - whistle down to earth.

Earlier, during the blitz, tons of scrap iron had smashed greenhouses and tiles, sometimes narrowly missing someone who had been foolish enough to be out of the shelters. The enemy bombs had fallen short, and the remains of the rockets had done the main damage. But it was wonderful for morale to see them in the night sky. And so we had spent the year, fifty men, twenty-five women of the ATS, three subalterns, a captain and a major.

So here I am back again. Anti-aircraft command has disgorged the young and fit and we are off to the banana boat. There are two possibilities. Is it to be Burma, or the Middle East? We know it will be warm - we have bought our khaki-drill from Moss Bros, the Army and Navy and Allkit. Absurdly long khaki 'shorts'. Puttees with a strange ribbon of khaki to attach them over our boot tops. Long socks, baggy ill-cut tunics - only the solar topee is missing. We could otherwise look like the defenders of Spion Kop. We have all tried the kit on at home, but now it is stowed away, not wanted on the voyage to who knows where. And we are tramping through the grey, wet streets in the Liverpool dawn through Lime Street to the docks.

It has been a sleepless night. As I march along with the twenty men in my draft who will be my responsibility for the next few weeks, I recall another day in Liverpool. Back to the hot summer of 1943. A Wings for Victory Parade. We must raise the morale of the population. And so we march through the streets, contingent after contingent. The Navy, Engineers, Home Guard, Artillery and Air Force. The people stand in their thousands and cheer. We feel good. The bands play and we puff out our chests.

But today, we are loaded with our full packs, and there is no cheering. The women are on their way to work at the factories. They stand and watch us in silence. One or two wish us good luck, but as they stand and stare we see that a few of them are silently weeping.

I think of my old father, another generation, and how he marched to a troopship thirty years ago for Mesopotamia and the campaigns against the Turks. Yes, I knew a good deal about war. But so far real war had been second hand. Father's stories of Lawrence were another echo from the past. I had at least had our wonderful year at Oxford, even if I got the chop. One year, staircase twelve in the second quad at Jesus. And old Alf my scout had been Lawrence of Arabia's servant. 'Keep away from the women' my father had said - almost his last words. I reflected that Lawrence hadn't had to bother, but then, I had mistakenly been dubbed 'Normal John'. Tucked away in my so-new officer's valise were my attestation paper and that extraordinary mistake made by the old pen-pushing Sergeant Major who had taken me before the Colonel, a volunteer, to take the oath. Normal John - Thank God I was normal! A catch phrase, a starter for undergraduate talk. 'Thank God I am normal', John Coyte would say in the Junior Common

Room at Jesus and we were away. What happens to the normal man under fire, I wondered?

Soon I would find out. Rockets and Liverpool had been something of a phoney war. Living in a suburban billet with Major Jenkins, Captain Kirk, Joe Radford and the men and ATS around the cycle stadium, weekends had been fun. As we marched past the opening to the Mersey tunnel I recalled those Sundays in Liverpool coming back with a misfire in the lorry. The whole of the tunnel closed, just for me, the Sergeant Major and a dozen men back from practice, firing our rockets at Kirkby.

Through we'd go, the fire engine stationed at one end of the tunnel, the ambulance at the other end and a three-ton lorry and our misfires in the back. But that was all in the past. Now we were off to the real war.

'This will sort the men out from the boys' said Corporal Cunningham. Privately I hoped that if the men were the ones who didn't return I would be one of the boys.

On down Church Street. It was here that I'd been accosted for the first time in my life by a big, black pimp. 'Do you play the piano?' he said.

'Indeed, yes' I replied.

'Would you like to play the piano with my sister? he asked.

It was then that I speculated on the colour of the keyboard and hastily turned the offer down. I was young and innocent of such things. A year of geography at Oxford had taught me more about the sextant than sex and I knew the geology of the Weald better than the geography of women.

And so on to the docks. The largest boat I'd ever sat in was a punt on the Cherwell, but there the only hazard had been Parson's Pleasure. 'You'll have to get out Mary, while I punt her past the Pleasure'. Two or three naked Bacchi sunning themselves. But there would be other hazards for us this time. 'Officers up the gangway'. 'Conducting officers report to the purser's office', then 'fallout on the dockside'.

The grey Liverpool morning is turning to rain. We are on board. We wonder how many of us will return and how the dice will be cast in this lottery of life and death. *Dulce et decorum est pro patria mori.*

Life on board a ship as a passenger is lived in a condition of suspended animation. There is nothing he can do to change its direction or make it go faster or more slowly. In this state of limbo between the two worlds of departure and arrival, he is lifted out of time. There is an added flavour when he knows not his destination or his expected time of arrival and a particular piquancy when there is, in wartime, a chance that he will not arrive at all.

Two years had now passed since reading geography at university, so the frustration of an unknown course and landfall was not inconsiderable. In the officers' mess in Liverpool, as something of an amateur meteorologist, I had, for the past years, been blamed for the vagaries of the weather. Friends in the RAF who were 'met' men complained of the same thing. The weather is uncertain and we all need a whipping boy. And so it was that at sea, knowing something of the sextant, the sun's altitude, the longitude and time but without the means to make more than intelligent guesses, I was threatened with fates of unpleasant varieties from friends who in every sense were as much at sea as myself. At one stage it was, however, clear that we had travelled a considerable part of the way to America, whilst at another the dolphins and flying fish seemed to hint that we might really be on the road to Mandalay! All this, however, lay in the future.

CHAPTER ONE

'We're here because we're here because we're here because we're here we're here because we're here because we're here because we're here' echoes again from the past. The humble soldier on active service spends a good deal of his time not knowing where he is or where he is going. The war for which we were bound was a war of movement; we would not lay our heads long in any place for any length of time. Today we live in a world of some certainty, at least about our geographical location on the morrow. But then we slept in haystacks, billets, slit trenches, tents, here today and gone tomorrow. We led the life of the hobo, but unlike him we were men under authority. The peacetime soldier trades some of his freedom for his bread and butter. Voluntarily or involuntarily, we had traded all of ours for the duration. But there was a certain spice in this. It is just a little exciting not to know where you are going. This was a mystery tour to end all mystery tours. We were off to war, and there would be a good deal of excitement before we saw Liverpool - or home – again.

A new experience always imprints itself vividly upon the mind. In the first place, most of those who travelled with us in the *Samaria* as it made its way to join the great convoy off the Western Approaches had never been to sea. Unlike the sophisticated traveller of today, the British soldier in World War II was a relatively untravelled man. If he had been fortunate he would have enjoyed an annual family holiday at the seaside. If, like myself, he had been a Midlander, he would have been lucky even to have done that. There were many aboard who had never been to the coast, apart from a day trip. There were few indeed who had ventured on to the open ocean, and almost none who had voyaged before in a vast company of ships in wartime.

CHAPTER ONE

The sight of a mighty convoy at sea, even for the experienced traveller, is a great wonder. As we awoke on that first morning from our bunks and emerged on deck, we began to have some idea of the immense organisation and extent of purpose of which we were part. To date we had, most of us, seen it in a sort of microcosm. We had lived in our own small world on gun sites in anti-aircraft command, being posted here and there, usually in units of a few dozen or a hundred men. Down the ages the soldier has always spent much of his time in such conditions. In our fathers' war it had only been in the great set pieces - the Somme, Passchendaele, Verdun, when in a mighty offensive the total purpose of the whole had seemed to merge with the routine of life in the troop, the platoon or the company. And so the vast convoy, stretching from horizon to horizon, reflected for us the macrocosm of the world conflict in which we were playing our small part.

Apart from the great variety of ships - destroyers, aircraft carriers with their planes perched on deck, cruisers, cargo vessels of every sort and size, passenger liners like our own *Samaria*, filling their wartime role of troopship, the outstanding impression was one of a uniform grey. The sea was grey, the ship was grey, the other ships were painted in their wartime grey and a number of our fellow passengers were greyer than all of them. The ship had recently provisioned in America and food was generous by wartime standards. But as I sat at the table on the first morning for breakfast, the fried egg slid in the fat from side to side of the plate and my companion, Jack Midgeley, turned grey himself and asked me if I would like his breakfast whilst he took a turn on deck.

Conditions below on the troop decks were rather worse. And so we took our turns for fresh air on this extraordinarily crowded boat. Destroyers moved up and down the convoy, lights flashed from time to time and the mighty concourse of ships made its way westwards. We were aware that the U-boat offensive had now largely been contained, but nevertheless there were anxious times ahead. We had a lively understanding of our vulnerability, in spite of the awesome protection afforded by the Fleet. In wartime the most precious convoys of all were those that carried the armies of trained soldiers to the battlefronts, and our respect for the professional skills of the Navy was unbounded.

The days were punctuated by meals which were, for the officers at least, more generous than most of us had seen in the war - and in some cases in our lives. The hungry 1930s had given way to the rationed forties and we lived, it seemed, like kings. The NAAFI, stocked with unlimited supplies of Hershey's milk chocolate, kept us going between what seemed to be gargantuan meals, though they were in reality no more generous than our children would enjoy later from the supermarket shelves of the seventies. But below decks the men were crowded in tiered bunks and hammocks in an atmosphere that seemed little less foetid than the slavers of two centuries past. No wonder that by day the decks were crowded to the point where on one occasion when the destroyer began to put down smokescreens, everyone rushed over to one side to see what was happening, and the whole vessel took a distinct list to port,

The days passed uneventfully. We began to censor the mail and each evening I was handed a bunch of letters by my sergeant major, which would then disappear into the hands of the Army Post Office after we had completed the task of basic censorship. As well as SWALK - sealed with a loving kiss - we began to find ITNLY (I Trust aNd Love You) frequently appearing in the correspondence, and we began to wonder if the bush telegraph might perhaps be tuned to the correct frequency. Seven years at grammar school and a first year up at Oxford had cut me off in some degree from much of the education systems of those days and the literacy of the common soldier extended over a wide range. At one end of this was the gypsy who was to join my platoon later in the 8th Army and with whose wife I conducted a lively correspondence over a period of some months. Not only was he unable to write, but he could not to compose a letter and his wife, similarly, retained a scribe at the other end. The scribe and I, consequently, corresponded and the letters were dutifully read out to the main parties as we received them in the army mail. In many of the letters which I read as I expunged, the occasional references to expected destination and often classified material touched the heart. Many parted for ever on embarkation leave, and many of our companions had left behind young wives and sweethearts.

The generation that went to war in the forties was better informed than that of 1914. We knew that the expected life of an infantry man was but a few months and of a platoon commander even less. We knew uncles, friends of our parents, neighbours who had lost a limb, an eye or worse in that dreadful affair and there were few amongst us who did not from time to time have dark thoughts of the future. But we have, fortunately, a strangely protective personal philosophy which covers the soft shell of the psyche with a carapace of comfort. Getting killed or wounded is something that happens to someone else, or at least that was what many of us told ourselves.

One man had already died unaccountably on board from a bullet from his own rifle and another had shot himself in the foot. And the fatalism of the shell with your name written upon it caused others to hope that all those missiles awaiting them in the arsenal of the enemy had indeed been stamped and addressed with names and destinations other than their own.

As we rode south-west gently down the Gulf Stream Drift, the weather became warmer and the men were glad to escape from the foul and overcrowded atmosphere below decks. The order was posted for us to don our new khaki drill, and so we became latter-day 'gentlemen in khaki going south'. The British soldier is a born gambler, and amongst his number there are inevitably a few speculative entrepreneurs who scent a fertile field of potential personal profit. As if from nowhere sets of housey-housey cards (today called Bingo) appeared, and inevitably the meagre pay of the many began to flow into the ample pockets of a few. Had we been torpedoed and the survivors drifted to a desert island, human nature would, I am sure, have produced in the long run a capitalist rather than a socialist society!

As for the officers, it became clear that there were two distinct classes: those who played bridge and those who did not. I had always found card games something of a bore, so I sought out those many amongst our company who like myself had had a year at the University. We sat on deck and speculated about our own fate and the great conflict in which we were to play our small part. The pattern of the war had in many cases dictated that paths were to cross frequently. This is a common experience of servicemen. I sought out Dickie Henson and Antony Franklin, who had been with me at Jesus as an exhibitioner. As earlier related, Antony had awards at both Cambridge and at Oxford, but had had to turn down his first prize at Cambridge as his parents, kind and humble folk from

Rugby, had not had the wherewithal to supplement his scholarship sufficiently to enable him to go up. As Headmaster of a big day school which sent young men by the hundred to the universities, I could but think how lucky they were compared with our generation.

Antony had fortunately gained another award at Oxford at a less expensive college and had already gained a First in his part I in one year of study. He was talented and had already written verse of distinction. He was to die a few weeks before the war ended in Northern Italy. Dickie, intended for the church, was to be mortally wounded in the Gothic line offensive, of which more later.

We had all served as young subalterns in AA command and had spent the previous two months at Dunbar in Scotland on the Lammermuir Hills, preparing for the change over to infantry regiments. There was sound reason for such a redeployment of about a thousand young officers, but the process was initiated by the War Office with sad ineptitude. Men, often from pre-war Territorial Army units, were sent with little notice and no reason given to retrain. There were ugly rumours of discontent.

In January 1944 the Adjutant General was sent from London to Dunbar to address the first draft of 500 young officers. The whole Officers' Training Unit convened in a local cinema and His Majesty's Adjutant General was shouted down. The matter never reached the press, for it was wartime, but things could have been better handled. In World War II officers were not simply content to do or die, they wanted to know the reason why.

Things settled down after a while and with weekend leave possible at the Officers' Club in Queen Street, Edinburgh, morale improved. Dickie and I recalled one of those weekends when we had walked along Princes Street behind a major in his British Warm accompanied by a striking young woman. In those days of clothes rationing women had, with their ancient guile and resource, found other things with which to adorn themselves. Only the Americans produced silk stockings, otherwise you could get leg paint in various shades of tan. On the back of the major's British Warm was the distinct imprint of the legs of his companion, angled in such a way that it was clear that they had had a very happy weekend. We were a spirited lot of young men. After the hard training with live ammunition on the Lammermuir Hills, we had at last departed for embarkation leave. As the troop train left Dunbar station, on which stood the commandant and his staff and the discomfited Adjutant General sent up again from Whitehall, all hell broke loose. Very pistols were fired, thunderflashes flew from carriage windows, bursts of tracer shot up to the sky and smoke canisters enveloped the train and station in a dense cloud. The platform party rapidly took cover in the waiting rooms and lavatories, and we felt that we had at least left our mark behind us.

But now all this was past, and we faced a sterner test. As we sat on the deck of the *Samaria* in the late afternoon, the sun set behind us in the west. The great convoy had turned towards the north-east and we were heading for the Straits of Gibraltar. Two days later, as night fell, we passed between the rock and Tangier.

It was to be a night passage, for we were only too well aware that each convoy passing through the Straits was soon reported back to German Fighter Command by local land-based agents. We were soon to be made uncomfortably aware of the result of the information they had passed.

The feelings experienced by a passenger on a ship at hazard are, I suppose, not unlike those of a passenger on an aircraft in trouble. An infantryman on his own two legs at least has some control over his circumstances. He has some choice of cover and something to do. But a passenger on a ship must accept his fate and has no control over his immediate destiny.

We were below decks in the ship's theatre listening to a well-known dance band leader of pre-war vintage who was playing the piano to an enthusiastic audience. Suddenly there came the call to boat station. There was no panic. As we emerged above decks in our life jackets, the ship shuddered as depth charges went over the side from neighbouring destroyers. Others steamed up and down the convoy emitting smoke screens around the precious troopships. I cannot recall that any of us admitted to being scared - I don't think we were. The whole ship listed to port as men dashed to the side to watch, and we had to quite literally redress the balance. It was all very exciting, and we had a boundless confidence in the competence of our naval escort. At this stage of the war the U-boats were far fewer in number and we came through unscathed. But I suppose that in some corner of the mind of each one of us was a judgment upon our own reaction to this first mortal danger which must presage the shape of things to come in the months ahead.

During the course of the next few days the convoy seemed to gain speed. The weather was already hot. One day a solitary locust landed on board the ship from the African coast to our south which we were hugging under the air cover of a now friendly coastline. Then one afternoon half our company steamed on to Suez, while we turned north. We knew then, for the first time, that our enemy was to be a European one. The treatment the Japanese had meted out to prisoners of war and the conditions of jungle warfare were not relished by many of us, and it was with some relief that we now knew we were to be reinforcements for the Allied armies knocking at the gates of Cassino.

The following morning we woke to find ourselves steaming gently past that incomparable approach to a landfall on a spring morning, the Bay of Naples. In this modern age of sophisticated travel it is not easy to describe the impact of strange places upon the young men of those days at the heart of a great adventure. For this indeed heightened our experience. As I have said before, few had been further than the nearest seaside town and this strange coastline with the hilltops clad with umbrella pines and cypresses shimmering in the gathering heat with old Vesuvius in the background was not to be forgotten. Later we were to see something of the immediate results of the 1944 eruption.

Substantial parts of the dock facilities were unusable at this stage of the war as a result of demolition, and as the troopship moved close to the harbour mole we were told that unloading was to be done by lighters. The hold was opened and nets operated by the ships' cranes carried men, equipment and baggage on a merry ride from the depths of the ship onto the attendant small craft. The process of unloading took most of the day and the waiting three-ton lorries on the shore began to move our stores and troops inland to an unknown destination. The officers remained aboard the ship till last. There had been a few stray night raids of late on the docks by Foggia based aircraft and we hoped - as indeed did the crew aboard *Samaria* - to have all done by dark.

Towards evening we became increasingly aware of the

thunder of distant guns, and as darkness began to fall we became aware of the flashing of lights along the horizon to the north. The great battle for Cassino was on, and few among us were unaware of what lay ahead. A cargo vessel was unloading in the dusk not far away onto one of the lighters. I looked over the side as we prepared to leave the ship. 'I think they're coffins' said Antony. But he was not to occupy one for nearly another year. We had seen Naples; the real war lay ahead.

CHAPTER TWO

INFANTRY REINFORCEMENTS

On that night early in May 1944 as we disembarked, the war in Europe was at a turning point. There, can, of course, never be any doubt that the Russians had carried the main burden of the land conflict. Their communist friends at home had been calling for many months for a second front in Europe, but they had been in no way anxious to open one in the East to relieve Britain when she stood alone in 1940. And indeed, we already had our second front in Italy. But the so-called 'soft underbelly' of the Axis powers was proving to be a bony morsel to chew. The great battle for Cassino was still raging and as we moved northwards, after disembarkation through the warm Italian night, we could hear the distant thunder of the guns at the front. Yet further north, General Lucas's 'stranded whale', as Churchill had described it, still floundered at Anzio (where the beachhead had been established in an attempt to outflank Cassino and take Rome), whilst at home, the great armies of invasion were gathering in the coastal regions of southern England.

We live today in an age when communications are open and information is immediate and readily available. This was not so during wartime in the 1940s. As lorry after lorry rolled northwards with its cargo of troops, we had no idea where we were bound; for all we knew we were to be thrown into the conflict the following day. However, after a couple of hours, or perhaps less, the convoy halted and we stepped out into the warmth of the Italian night. A mobile kitchen dispensed meat and vegetable soup into our mess tins and we were conducted to an encampment in an olive grove, where tents awaited us. It had been a long day and we unrolled our valises and slept soundly on the dry dust.

On the main road from Naples to Benevento, where a fortunate unit of the 8th Army had recently liberated the Strega liqueur factory, is a right turning into a winding country road, in those days dusty and unmetalled, which leads to the large village of Cervinara. Strung along the road are the satellite hamlets of Paolisi, Rotundi and San Martino. The whole complex lies in a fertile plain covered with olive groves and vineyards and flanked on both sides by Apennine foothills. The purple mountain mass of Taburno looks down upon this pastoral scene. Irrigation channels criss-cross the smallholdings, donkeys walk, blindfolded in circles drawing water from the local wells, women in black trudge along in the dust of the roadside bearing amphorae of fresh water to the villages. The hot summer sun shines from an unbroken blue sky upon this idyllic landscape, and no imagination was needed in those days to accept that the scene had changed little from century to century. It was among this group of villages that the army had decided to locate the Infantry Reinforcement Training Depot of the British Italian forces.

I cannot help returning again to a theme which I am sure will be echoed and well understood by others upon their first visiting foreign places in the two world wars. On that May morning my letter home reflected the experience of my father in another conflict. In his turn in 1915 he had gone to Bombay to acclimatise, and later to Mesopotamia. How often had I looked, as a boy, through the faded photographs he had brought back with him and listened to his tales of gunboats on the Tigris and the hardships of the war against the Turks. But most of all, through his old soldier's tales, came the wonder of seeing new places in India and the desert oases of the river valleys of Iraq. Like others of his kind and times, a poorly paid shopkeeper's assistant in a Midland town, foreign travel had been an impossible dream.

He had, as related, returned from the wars to set up his own business, and the crash of 1929 had left him bankrupt. So it was my mother, a village schoolmistress, who kept the family together through his years of unemployment in the hungry thirties. For my sister and me, foreign travel had been out of the question. So it was that, along with many thousands of others and our father before me, the impact of a foreign place, substantially different from home, was immediate and powerful. The sophisticated young of today, brought up on colour television, cheap air fares and glossy magazines, can have little understanding of the stimulus of all this upon an earlier generation.

Since those far off days I have travelled widely, but I have never forgotten that first day in a foreign place, our senses heightened as they were by the dangers that lay so close to us at the front. Hanging is said to concentrate the mind wonderfully, and many who have lived, often at hazard, in war have in common that vivid recollection of events and places. It is as if the senses are working overtime to imprint themselves clearly should one of them be arrested forever by loss of sight, hearing or worse on the field of battle.

But of all the senses the one which is most evocative, and which in memory precipitates nostalgia best, perhaps because it is the most primitive, is that of smell. This was never more so than in these ancient villages of Calabria to which I was to return many years after the war. A combination of heat and the lack of drainage and other facilities combined to produce a distinctive odour which, once encountered, reawakens buried memories ever afterwards, far more effectively than sight or sound.

The small village of Paolisi, which was nearest to our encampment in the olive groves, comprised a narrow road only wide enough for a single vehicle to pass and flanked on either side by the heavy timbered street doors so common in southern places. Balconies overhung this already constricted passageway and the rooms which opened on to the street often contained a bed, down upon which gazed the portraits of the Virgin Mary and President Roosevelt in the place of honour most recently vacated by that of Signor Mussolini. Chickens ran in and out, and some of the humble homes had been converted into small shops selling walnuts and oranges or offering a free laundry service in exchange for bars of soap. A couple of the more attractive houses had been appropriated by the army and converted into an officers' mess.

As we sat down for our first meal we were assailed by a host of houseflies. They were everywhere. The air was full of them and only the heat of the food deterred them from landing upon it. The rim of each plate was black with insects, and as each mouthful cooled on the fork they attempted to settle upon it before it could reach our mouths. The reason for this soon became apparent when we ventured into the back lanes and alleyways of the village, which all seemed to provide open air public facilities.

As I sat quietly in the branches of an olive tree a few days later with a rifle, an old lady in black settled on the ground beneath me, lifted her voluminous skirts and proceeded to answer the more demanding call of nature. When she heard me move above her, she glanced up. Completely unembarrassed, she bade me a friendly good morning!

No doubt the local inhabitants were able to resist any effects upon their digestive systems from the continuous traffic of flies between food and excreta, but we were more vulnerable and before long acute enteritis was the daily lot of many of the Allied soldiery. Each unit, therefore, sought various solutions to the problem. Perhaps one of the more spectacular was that adopted by some neighbouring Royal Engineers. The local mayor was sent for by the Commanding Officer, together with other *prominente*, and paraded in the village square. It was pointed out that the village was ill-equipped with the necessary facilities, apart from the homes of his worship the village priest and one or two other families of good standing. The gallant colonel then drew his revolver, pointed it at the mayor and made it abundantly clear that within 24 hours each family in the village would be expected to build a latrine to a standard specification; a pit three feet wide and six feet deep. His fierce demeanour and the display with the revolver left the mayor in no doubt that both his life and that of other village worthies might well be at risk if the work was not completed, and completed on time.

The *Tedeschi* (Germans) had not long departed from the area, and such threats were not to be taken lightly in a community so recently at hazard from fascist overlords. There was feverish activity. Men were called in from olive grove and vineyard and as the night came they disappeared underground.

Planking was obtained and the pits were shored up as each family frantically dug down into the stony ground. Throughout the night the village was dotted with lights and the air was filled with the sound of pick and shovel.

To the astonishment of the Engineers as they walked around the village on the following day, some of the pits were already far deeper than the requisite six feet. As the time approached for the colonel's inspection of the works, a weeping mayor asked for an interview and an extension of' the time permitted for their completion. It soon became apparent that a mistake had been made and that six feet had been interpreted as six metres.

Work ceased. The ladders were hauled up from the pits and the terrified mayor realised that the threat of an early death had been lifted from him. The engineers demonstrated how a rough shelf of planking could complete the specification.

Unfortunately, after a few weeks, the flies were as bad as ever; few, if any, of the villagers had felt themselves able to defile their beautifully excavated latrines. It is difficult to adopt a new pose when you have always answered the call of nature in the more natural way. The only pit that was ever filled was occupied one night by a fat mule, which stumbled into it and got stuck at its waistline, waking the village with its frantic bellowing. As the colonel said as he looked at the pristine emptiness of the pits, 'You can take a horse to water, but you can't make him drink!'

And so it was that we lived with houseflies for companions by day and mosquitoes by night. But the flies, as we were to see, became more sinister as we moved nearer the battle front.

As we left the mess after that first meal and walked along the dusty track back to our tents, we passed the Sawyer stoves and other cooking facilities of the army kitchen. Strung along the roadside in an expectant queue was a ragged line of urchins, each carrying a large tin can, some with wire handles attached. Most were barefoot, some were emaciated and all were hungry. The whole densely-populated region of southern Italy had had its communications completely disrupted since the invasion at Salerno. The battlefront had cut the country in half and food imports for the local population had been almost non-existent. The economy of the country was disrupted and inflation was raging. In this situation a flourishing black market had grown up, which I shall describe later.

As always, in times of shortage and trouble, the weakest go to the wall. This was exacerbated in a part of the country where hunger was, and often still is, the lot of the poor at the best of times. There were nevertheless adequate quantities of cheap, rough wine, though food was in short supply for our Italian hosts. The British soldier of those days, like the British public at large, was accustomed to quenching his thirst with beer when he could afford it.

Upon my attestation I had been handed four shillings for two days' pay and my first pay parade as a cadet had yielded five shillings after an hour's wait, with half a crown immediately impounded for barrack damages by the Regimental Sergeant Major. Even in 1942 it was difficult to provide much opportunity for alcoholic excess from such wages. Nevertheless, for the first time in their lives many of our men discovered that they could consume substantial quantities of cheap alcohol from their army pay.

On entering a bar they would ask for wine and upon being given a bottle and glasses would request larger containers and proceed to swig the stuff down as they would have consumed mild ale at home. As each new draft arrived it fell to the lot of their officers to tour the district with a three-ton lorry and pick up the drunks from the local bars and wine shops. This period of alcoholic acclimatisation resulted in many sore heads, fights and attendant problems as the demon vino took its toll. The drinking inevitably led to other excesses, and as occasional leave became possible in Naples, as I shall describe later, some of the more licentious soldiery contracted venereal disease.

I was later to inherit a Roman Catholic batman who would contract a series of doses and spend a few days in hospital, followed by a religious retreat organised by the RC padre at which he presumably repented for his excesses!

Other precautions also had to be taken. Anti-malarial mepacrine tablets were prescribed daily and mosquito nets by night were still required. Although Mussolini, the bullfrog of the Pontine marshes, had supposedly disposed of the anopheles mosquito, there was still some residual malarial danger at that time in the deep south of the country.

The summer of 1944 in Italy was a hot one even by local standards. The olive groves around us were shrill with the matinee concert of the violin section of the cicada orchestra and their pizzicato. At night, the crack-crack bass of the bulllfrog chorale took, over and in the darkness the fireflies illuminated the arena. Like all who served in the Mediterranean theatre, we were conscious of the great white wheel of the Milky Way, and the velvet warmth of the night was bright with stars. Much of our training was done in the hours of darkness, for this would provide us with experience of the work of the front-line soldier, so often done at night. Steep hillside terraces, irrigation canals and mountain slopes can offer substantial hazards after dark, and as we moved about our business, particularly when the moon was not full or had not yet risen, we had several casualties. The peasants knew their country better.

One night we set out soon after dusk. After several hours climbing and tactical exercising en route, we found ourselves at dawn on top of Mount Ciesco, 1350 metres high. To our astonishment, three old ladies in black had reached the summit before us from the village, each carrying on her head a full basket containing several kilos of oranges. They were soon to be disposed of at about three times the retail price then current in the local shops.

Training proceeded apace, frequently with live ammunition. Having trained initially at Oxford as a field gunner, been commissioned in anti-aircraft and worked on rockets and now in the infantry, I found there were few weapons with which I was not conversant. We fired Very pistols, became proficient with our revolvers and spent an interesting afternoon shooting tin cans off a wall. We used captured enemy weapons and learnt a good deal about their sounds and characteristics.

One afternoon in the square at Cervinara we were practising with a two-pounder anti-tank gun. A senior officer walked up to the sergeant-instructor. 'I hope you have impressed upon these gentlemen that this is a weapon to be handled with care' he said. He picked up a round of ammunition and opened the breech. 'You must always load the gun with a clenched fist' he said. 'If you extend your fingers like this there is every chance that you may lose one of them as the breech block springs up automatically when the round is loaded. ' Upon saying this he pushed the round up the spout. The breech block came up - and off came his finger.

'Has anyone got a handkerchief?' he asked. One was

produced and the blood was staunched. He then picked up his own finger from the dry dust, licked it clean, popped it into his handkerchief, put it in his pocket and walked off to see the medical officer. After a few yards he fainted. We all voted it the most thorough demonstration we had seen to date.

Training continued throughout the ensuing weeks. We moved up the valley from Paolisi to Cervinara and later to San Martino. At each encampment, battle-experienced men from the line put us through new routines. We unlearned a great deal that we had learned back at home. There is no substitute for battle experience, and so we came to know some of the grisly tricks of the trade of the infantryman and the ways he may better survive.

Rome fell, and along with some more adventurous souls I was able to get a few days' leave and follow the army north nearly to the front itself. When I returned to San Martino I met Antony Franklin as I walked into the mess for dinner. He handed me a paper. We were both under orders to move northwards to join our regiments in the front line.

CHAPTER THREE

INTO BATTLE

There are some experiences in life which can only with the greatest difficulty be communicated to others who have not shared in them. Amongst these must be that of childbirth, which can only be the lot of women, the unique and unimaginable detachment from his home planet of the space traveller and the nightmare memories of prisoners who have lain in the concentration camps of the evil dictatorships of our century. Along with these, I believe, are the experiences of men in battle.

The Western Front in 1914-1918 has been well documented in prose and in verse. The unique quality of verse can with more certainty communicate to a later generation an understanding of the human experience of the stress of battle. The Second World War produced much less verse of distinction than that of 1914-1918. One simple explanation of this is probably that the long, static conflict of the First World War trenches was not repeated in the second, and that the experience of most soldiers was in shorter spells as part of a war of movement. Nomadism is less conducive to writing. There can however be no doubt that those who were so involved were aware of an experience their fathers had shared in 1914-1918. And those who have walked through the valley of the shadow of death, losing some good companions upon the way, find the sunlight all the sweeter when the shadows depart on the morrow.

The land that lies just behind the lines in warfare is a strange one. The usual rules do not apply. There is nothing straightforward or simple or ordered in its communications and customs. Here, normal life as we know it is suspended as the rule of military law replaces the rule of law itself. So it is that homes and farms are commandeered, pigs and chickens sometimes end up in the pots of the finders, cows and goats are milked, to their great relief, as the army marches along on its stomach.

The reaction of the local populace as we moved northwards through their vineyards and olive groves was always that the Tedeschi had taken everything. The Eighth Army had, by this time, become a polyglot force, but generally speaking the British soldier behaved himself well. It was more often with relief that we were received as we occupied towns and villages on our way.

The land behind the lines is not always a particularly safe place, and this was more so in the second war than the first. The front was always to some degree fluid, and although we had air superiority we were subjected to occasional visitations. One night when we were resting before battle to the east of Rimini I had arrived late at night and unrolled my valise in a camouflaged tent beside a battery of guns in the unit cookhouse. During the night I awoke to hear an aircraft low overhead, and before we could rouse ourselves a hail of bullets swept through the cookhouse and buried themselves in the ground. We see many films today on television in which such events are commonplace, but the direct experience of being strafed from the air is most alarming. Fortunately no one was hurt.

There is also the cold and deadly danger of minefields which are as yet uncleared. At a later stage in the campaign I had the task of running a mobile soup kitchen for a couple of days for men who were out of battle. All was peaceful, so a friend and I decided to walk out one afternoon for a swim from a nearby beach close to Gaeta. We strolled over the sands for some considerable distance and stripped out and swam.

As we changed back into our khaki drill I pointed out to him a chunk of metal projecting from the sand. It was a German Tellermine (plate mine). These anti-tank mines were not likely to explode unless pressed by a heavy track or wheel, but then we looked more carefully around us and saw the antenna of a German anti-personnel mine projecting nearby. These could cut a man in half.

In spite of the cooling swim we both began to sweat. We followed our own footsteps out from the minefield and across the dunes. When we reached the road both of us were dripping with perspiration. Further along, partly obscured by some vines, a German sign saying 'Achtung, Minen' stood intact. In spite of the heat of the day and the sweat I suddenly felt cold, and as I looked at my companion I could see that his hair was actually standing away from his scalp.

The presence of danger and consequent fear do not exist in direct proportion to one another. The soldier can be in deadly peril and yet be calm and collected under fire. He can, on the other hand, lose his nerve and become shattered and shell-shocked after the battle has passed him by. The psychology of fear and its attendant effects upon the individual are unpredictable. It was possible to sleep soundly with shells passing overhead in both directions – 'outgoing and incoming mail', as we called them - yet to lie up in an agony of fear, heart beating fast, on night patrol with all silent and just the faint smell of a corpse drifting in on the night breeze as a reminder of one's own fragile humanity.

Much of the burden of war which we as infantrymen carried lay in the weight that could press upon our minds and imaginations in our night thoughts. Activity, physical or mental, was a great relief. The officer or NCO who has much to ponder for his men, his maps to read, his signals to send, his concern for rations, his orders to take and pass on, has, in many respects, a better day. The private has more time to ponder upon his fears, the death of a comrade and the mutilation he has witnessed, fates which could on the morrow come his own way.

But night fears were common to all and nightmares the lot of many. Even my great and courageous father-in-law, Bill Afford, who was recommended

for the VC in Colonel Mobbs' sportsmen's battalion of the Northamptonshire Regiment in 1914-18 and who got the DCM as a consolation prize, had nightmares of the front long after the end of that fearful holocaust. It was also well recognised in World War II that men had a breaking point, and after a long period of strain, lack of sleep and the persistent burden of fear of death or mutilation, even the most courageous could succumb.

The mental anguish and extortion of the very store of sanity of those who suffered at Passchendaele in 1917 was only rarely repeated in more isolated circumstances in the battlefields of the West and was probably more nearly approached at

Stalingrad, or, in different guise, in the hideous concentration camps of the Nazi régime. Periods in the line were shorter, reliefs more frequent. Nevertheless, most of us admitted privately to a steady erosion of our capital of moral courage, and recognised that it was a bank account with a diminishing income, eventually subject to being overdrawn.

The battlefield was not always quiet by night and much movement took place under cover of darkness. I recall vividly one such evening as I moved up towards the villages of Montescudo and Monte Colombo as the Eighth Army attempted, in the early autumn of 1944, to penetrate the Gothic Line in the northern Apennines and move into the Plain of Lombardy before the winter. Z Company of the 2nd/5th Battalion of the Hampshire Regiment had lain up during the previous day at part of the 46th London Division's attack of mid-September 1944 to break the back of the Gothic Line and move into the Po Valley before winter set in. We had spent the previous day in a vineyard south of Monte Colombo and a mobile canteen, manned by a kinswoman of General Sir Oliver Leese, had visited us. This was always a bad sign, well recognised by the men, for it had often meant in the past that we were soon to be in battle. Soon afterwards a Sten gun stuttered and a man was found to have a self-inflicted wound in his mouth. As night approached we loaded into RASC lorries. Like sheep travelling uncomfortably to the butchers along a modern motorway, we moved up towards the sound of the guns, which were already laying down a heavy barrage. The lorries took us to the areas which lay within the most extreme range of the enemy artillery, and here we debussed and marched north. On the horizon the shape of San Marino, looking like the fairy castles in the pre-war Gibbs toothpaste advertisements, gave the battlefield an eerie and almost medieval look as the sun set to the west.

We passed a motorcycle which had been flattened in the road by a tank; it had been spread to several times its original length and crushed almost into two dimensions. Soon afterwards we came to a Bren-gun carrier at a corner.

We halted for a rest on the march, and listened to the sound of shells passing overhead. 'Outgoing and incoming mail' said someone as the artillery from either side exchanged compliments. As we lay down in the gathering darkness there was a lively discussion about the possibility of two shells from opposite sides side colliding in mid air. We decided that the odds were remote. The British soldier is a great gambler, but before anyone could offer to open a book a shell fell uncomfortably close behind us and another to our front. A third arrived with no warning at all, as do all shells that fall dangerously close. There was a huge explosion, followed by the crackling of what appeared to be small arms fire at close range, without the crack and thump usually associated with it. After a few minutes it died down and we got back to our feet. The Bren gun carrier was badly damaged and it soon became clear that the shell had, by a miracle, landed inside it whilst the crew were stretching their legs. A box of ammunition had provided us with the fireworks and the walls of the carrier had taken the full blast.

As we continued along the road towards Monte Colombo, bursts of small arms fire criss-crossed from time to time in the night sky. The red of the British tracer contrasted with the white of that of the enemy as they stitched their lethal threads through the fabric of the night. In the distance one or two farms had caught fire, as the tracer had ignited stacks and storage barns, casting a baleful light over the battlefield and even at a distance causing us to feel badly exposed to more direct enemy fire.

We were glad to find some abandoned German slit trenches for temporary cover. They still smelt strongly of the enemy. Every army has its peculiar smell, probably compounded of its food supplies, the nature of its uniform and at times, as we were to find to our cost, its defecatory habits. Many are the good men who have been lost in the field with their trousers down, and the morning evacuation was often attended to at some peril. Fortunately, awareness of this frequently acted as a most excellent laxative, shortening the period during which one was at risk.

The extensive chain of fortified villages known as the Gothic Line had been excavated in large part by the Todt organisation, which used substantial slave labour from the German prison camps, including many prisoners of war from the Eastern front. We were not to know of the fearful fate of these unfortunates, who were later delivered into Stalin's hands for liquidation after the war ended. Later in this book I shall describe a meeting with Field Marshall Alexander, who had recently, in the summer of 1944, visited Winston Churchill, and who brought home to many of us for the first time the problem that lay ahead after the end of hostilities. I am reminded today of the limerick which goes:

> *There was an old fellow called Lenin*
> *Who did a large number of men in*
> *That's a lot to have done*
> *But for every one*
> *A fellow called Stalin did ten in.*

But in those days of our political innocence the 22,000 dead of Katyn still lay silent beneath the forest floor of Eastern Poland and the slave labour of Kolyma in Eastern Siberia had not yet communicated its message to the wartime world.

As we moved nearer to the front, we no longer found the carefully-excavated enemy slit trenches unoccupied. In their retreat a number of dead had been left behind and had remained unburied for some days. The sweet, sickly smell of a rotting corpse is one which all infantrymen have encountered down the ages, and it is a smell never forgotten. It awakens primitive sensations, inducing nausea and an awareness of the fragility of one's own existence. There is a strange sympathy which makes friend and foe kindred in the front line and the shadowy corpse of a blond Saxon youth in field grey lying dead in the weird half light reawakened our feelings of common identity. 'Poor little bastard' said Sergeant Manning.

We moved up towards Monte Colombo and at the top of the hill we found the door of a substantial building ajar. Z company filed inside the thick stone walls, where we settled down for the rest of the night to await further orders for the attack the following morning. The enemy had not long since departed and had left a downstairs room full of shit.

The moon rose, and during the night a corporal ventured outside to relieve himself. A few seconds later he hurried down the stairs to the basement in which we were sheltering.

'There's a tank outside!' he breathed.

'I didn't know we had any tanks up' said Major Kiddy.

A volunteer ascended the steps and peered out into the half light. It was an abandoned German tank. As dawn approached we moved off towards Montescudo. Opposite our night's shelter the Regimental Aid Post had taken up headquarters across the street. Outside the wall were a number of gas capes containing the remains of the recently dead. Again we were reminded, like all front-line soldiers, of the narrowness of the divide between the quick and the dead. As desultory shells fell close by from time to time we were quick to dive for cover.

We passed a cemetery and took up positions in trenches hastily excavated overlooking Trarivi. We established Z Company Headquarters in a half-ruined farmhouse and the platoon dug in around it. German movement was spotted in buildings in nearby Montescudo and we opened fire with a machine gun. Just after that, as I stood talking to Lt Jones in a slit trench, he fell dead, a sniper's bullet through his skull. He was a brave young man and had refused to wear his steel helmet in the line. The cloth cap marked him as an officer and he paid the price.

I was called forward with my orders group and as we moved from our cover and ran to the farmhouse a heavy shell fell amongst us. You never hear the one that hits you. A corporal lay dead beside me and Sergeant Manning was severely wounded in the back. There was no warning of the approaching heavy missile, only a huge explosion and an engulfing blast.

I lost consciousness for a time and came round later covered with much dust on a stretcher in the regimental aid post. There was a hazy recollection of riding in an ambulance under shellfire, and then everything faded. I awoke on the dockside at Ancona on a stretcher and within minutes we were loaded onto a hospital ship bound for Bari. For the first time for many days there was sleep.

Living today in our civilised society, there can be no one under the age of 85 who can recall the front line in the Second

World War. Few of us today spend days on end without sleep, unless we are insomniacs, and we no longer experience the desperate feelings of utter fatigue we knew in those far-off times. Nor is it easy to understand the relief of an opportunity simply to remove a pair of boots after days of wear, or to visit for the first time for weeks a mobile bath unit, or to savour a tin of meat and vegetables washed down with porridge and treacle and followed by canned American bacon after the rations have been delayed for days by shellfire and damaged roads. The intensity of such small pleasures is sorely missed in the care and comfort of our pampered lives, and it is no bad thing now and again to reflect upon the hardships of those times.

My own deep regret has always been for the good friends who did not survive and whose youth was cut off amid dangers and deprivations. They were never to know any rewards for their gallantry. The best and the bravest so often went to the wall, but at least the carnage of the Somme was not to be repeated, with the loss of the cream of a whole generation.

CHAPTER FOUR

TRANSIT CAMPS
AND TROOP TRAINS

To awaken on a late September morning in 1944 lying between clean sheets for the first time in six months, gently sailing down the Adriatic in a hospital ship, was a remarkable experience. I lay in a state of dreamlike euphoria in spite of the foul condition of my long-unwashed self, the murmurings of the seriously wounded and the night-time cries of those who still, in their sleep, were under shell fire. As I drifted in and out of consciousness as a result of the heavy injections, I became aware that a nurse was beside my cot. A tag was still attached to my wrist. My glasses had gone and as she felt my pulse she read it and said 'You've been very severely concussed, but you'll be all right. You've been unconscious for two days, but with rest and a check up we'll have you back with your unit in a week or two.

I remember that my main concern was with my filthy condition and the dust and mud I was depositing on the bed linen. 'We'll get you bathed at Bari' she added, 'we'll have to do a few checks'. Then I slid back into deep and unconscious exhaustion.

When next I came round, the rocking of the boat had ceased and I found myself in a military hospital in Trani. After a couple of days I was allowed to bath, and sat bunched up in a small tub in what had been until then a children's hospital, purpose built to scale. But all was not well. I walked from my little bath to the lavatory and the urine I passed was as black as soot. Back in the long ward, my skin soon changed to bright yellow. The severe concussion and partial burial in the derelict farm were not the only reasons for my weakness. Severe jaundice had set in, and for a couple of weeks I could eat no food. Although I did not know it at the time, acute enteritis was to lay me even lower, and with long weeks in hospital I was to lose three stones in weight. For me, effectively, the war's action was over.

As I sank lower and lower I did not really appreciate my own good fortune. A young officer in the next bed had lost a foot on a mine, and as he in turn rejoiced at his 'good luck' and news of severe casualties trickled back from friends in the regiment, it dawned upon me that I might, after all, survive the war. Luck plays a part in all our lives, but never more so than at such times.

Now I began to ponder this. If I had been selected by the sniper instead of young Jones a few feet away; if the shell had fallen two seconds earlier; if I had stepped a few inches to the right in a minefield... if, if, if. In matters of life and death it is so important to be the right man in the right place at the right time. Fortune had smiled. I had a debt to pay to her.

Military hospitals in wartime are not altogether depressing places. There are, of course, those who are critically wounded and who are on the point of death. But there are others who have received wounds from which they will recover, who have lost one of their less important appendages or who like myself were recovering after weeks of serious illness. The active war

40

for many of us was over, and for the first time for many years some of us began to plan for the future knowing that we would survive.

The nurses were kind and looked very beautiful, as was, perhaps, inevitable. It was not long before rumour circulated that our convalescent friends were visiting a single-bedded vacant ward from time to time. Matron could be fierce, as indeed could the senior medical officer, but we saw an unmistakable twinkle in their eyes on more than one such occasion.

My own journey to the little room at the end of the long ward was less pleasant. After a quick enema I was carried off for an encounter with the shuftiscope. I believe the medical profession call this peculiarly offensive instrument the sigmoidoscope. On the wall was a portrait of a huge black negro bending over, his rear amply displayed. It was indicated that this was the preferred posture and I was urged to comply. What seemed to be a piston rod from a large motor vehicle surmounted by an electric light bulb was, without ceremony, rudely thrust into my rear orifice and a motor horn was attached to the end. As they blew me up I recalled an unfortunate frog I had once seen inflated in a similar way by a boy at my village school. I also had a fleeting vision of the horror of the death of Richard II at the receiving end of a poker. The affair was very painful, and what they discovered in their interesting voyage I was not told. However, back to bed I went.

Gradually I regained my strength, and although I was still very thin and gaunt the sulfa drugs began to work and I was sent off to a convalescent home. This proved to be a quite luxurious hotel in Sorrento, in which I was allocated a bedroom of great magnificence. The painted ceiling was decorated with cherubs and other flying objects of religious mythology, and when I awoke in the mornings from the dark nights that so often haunt the front-line soldier, I could well believe momentarily that I had passed on to a happier place.

But the convalescent home was as good a billet as most of us had seen in years of soldiering. We were shown the local sights and the nurses accompanied us as we regained our strength. There were visits to Capri, to Axel Munthe's San Michaele, which we thought rather a phoney, and to Pompeii, where all was revealed, including the naughty murals in the brothel and the picture of the well-endowed gentleman weighing his testicles heavily in the scales against a pile of gold. 'They are worth more than their weight in gold' read the caption in Latin. Although there were some rather nasty wounds amongst those in our party, fortunately no one had lost that part of his anatomy and for these small mercies we were duly grateful.

On another day out we visited the love retreat of a latter-day Caesar, Signor Mussolini, and I will recount the story of that visit later in this book. I was also able to use this opportunity at Sorrento to replace some kit. My own had followed me down the line, but my valise had been slit open, presumably by our Italian friends in transit, and when it arrived everything had gone. I literally had nothing except a bed roll, my pyjamas, Red Cross bag and a borrowed battledress. Stealing from the sick and wounded and indeed the dead was an unhappy concomitant of war.

After a period of convalescence, during which the enteritis returned in bouts and I lost nearly three stone in weight, I was called before a medical board. There was a searching examination and a further encounter with the shuftiscope. It was decided that for six months I would be downgraded to medical Category B. My days as a front line soldier were over.

As Christmas of 1945 drew near, it was decided that I was now fit enough to do a job of work. My first assignment involved the running of a mobile soup kitchen for men as they came out of the line. The Italian railways had been substantially repaired up to Rome and Florence, and with a party of about 20 men recovering from light wounds we moved northwards with a fleet of three-ton lorries stuffed full of meat and vegetable soup for a prearranged point not far from Gaeta and south of Rome.

It was necessary first to contact the nearest town's mayor and find a place to live. It was now winter and raining incessantly. Unfortunately our rendezvous was at a junction in the old Adolf Hitler line, where most of the property had been destroyed by the heavy fighting before the breakout from Anzio. We eventually found a farmhouse which was relatively intact and which had been occupied by some nuns who had taken refuge from a damaged convent nearby. We moved the good women upstairs and commandeered the lower part of the buildings. They gratefully shared our meat and vegetable soup and gave us assistance in other ways. It was a happy arrangement, and the rude and licentious soldiery respected the ladies of the cloth. In general the British behaved well in occupied territories, and although the Italians in their chameleon ways welcomed each liberating group of the polyglot 8th Army with open arms as their saviours, I honestly believe that the solid qualities of the phlegmatic British soldier were respected more than those of most of our allies.

We set up our wash, dip and rinse facilities and made local requisitions of charcoal, and soon we had a continuous kitchen brewing up an appetising soup day and night. There were no train timetables and we were ready to feed the five thousand at all hours. The good sisters were in their element, and when at last we departed as the winter war became more static and there was movement behind the lines, they were sad to see us go.

Troop trains in wartime Europe had their own fascination. On one occasion I was going up to the front line from the railhead north of Naples. A deal of ancient rolling stock had been pressed into service and in this instance we were travelling in cattle trucks. Strict instructions were given about the danger of fire, and it was absolutely forbidden to brew up tea en route as there had been incidents in the past and cattle trucks were not provided with communication cords. The electric systems which powered the lines had been destroyed and the troop trains were hauled by American manned diesels.

From time to time the train would stop, the passengers would alight and small fires would be lit as the thirsty squaddies brewed up their tea. Men would then disappear into the olive groves and vineyards to answer the call of nature. The American soldiers would wait until many were so engaged and would then blow the whistle, and off would go the train pursued by the cursing British soldiery clutching their battledress trousers.

Early one morning we had stopped some distance south of Rome near Cassino. Men stepped off, washed and shaved and breakfasted. The first whistle blew and everyone got aboard except for one unpopular and unfortunate sergeant. His mirror was attached to the last cattle truck and he had delayed his ablutions. On the second whistle the train pulled sharply away, the doors were slammed and he was left razor in hand and soap on face dressed in pants and singlet.

He joined us some days later after an adventurous walk into

the next station down the line, clutching his razor. We heard later that he had had a most interesting interview with the local Railway Transport Officer.

As the winter war continued it became clear that the end was in sight and that arrangements must be made to deal with the movements of troops that would be required as Europe returned to peace. The port of Naples, in particular, had become the great entrepôt for men and supplies in to the Italian theatre, and it was decided that we should construct a huge encampment near Barra on the road to Pompeii to serve this purpose. The task was given to a unit which became known as X Special Reception Unit, stationed at Torre Annunziata at the foot of Vesuvius.

It was here that we spent the Christmas of 1945 in incessant rain, erecting barbed wire around the perimeter of the new encampment at Barra and wishing we were home. We did our best to cheer the men and ran a dance to which we invited what was known in those days as the local talent. On the appointed evening a motley collection of young ladies arrived, each accompanied by several chaperones in deepest black and mostly of great age. In spite of their fragile appearance they devoured enormous quantities of food and concealed the remainder within their voluminous skirts. The men enjoyed themselves, but contacts with the local ladies, other than the professionals, was of necessity superficial.

On Christmas Day we sat around a charcoal fire in the derelict farm we had occupied as a billet, drank to excess and watched the rain. I recalled earlier Christmases in the army. The war had seemed to go on for ever. I remembered the Christmas in Liverpool, when a group of urchins had sung a sweet carol outside the door of our billet. My officer commanding of those days, a Major Jenkins, a fierce Scot with a bristling moustache, listened to the first verses. He then marched to the door in his service dress and Sam Browne, his face ablaze with whisky and high blood pressure, and looked down at the tiny boys on the doorstep from his full six feet height.

They faltered to a halt in their last verse. 'Rushbridge!' he shouted to his batman, 'fetch my revolver!' Rushbridge disappeared for a moment, then came to the door and handed the weapon to the gallant OC. He cocked it and pointed it at the small boys. We all expected them to run, but they stood their ground. He felt in his pockets and handed them half a crown - a fortune for a Liverpool lad of those days. As he broke into a smile they wished us a merry Christmas and fled. But no one came to sing carols to us at Torre Annunziata. The only high spot of the day was when the Regimental Sergeant Major got drunk. This astonished us all. He had a vast capacity for alcohol and would usually appear on parade in the morning in close control of himself, sometimes swaying very gently rather like a lead-bottomed wobbly man as he gave his orders. But on this day he was felled. There had been a special ration of beer to celebrate the season and he had been long deprived of his native beverage. For the first time for many years he had been able to drink his fill. The ceremonial chamber pot had been passed around the sergeants' mess full of beer on Christmas Eve and he missed church parade on the morrow.

The camp which we started to construct in the new year, as the war moved towards its close, was called Lammie Camp after a general of that name. Covering many areas of vineyards on the coast road south of Naples, it was designed to accommodate troops embarking for shore leave, for release or for the war against Japan, which had not yet ended. Many of us anticipated that we would be sent to the Far East for that campaign. Across acres of farmland we constructed lines to sleep and feed thousands of men for short stays. A theatre, cinema, shop, church and recreation centres were built with locally-recruited civilian labour. I was appointed welfare officer, and with the assistance of Sergeant Harrington and Corporal Tattersall assumed my duties.

The local lads we employed caused us many problems. Two separate squads were given the task of cleaning the cinema and theatre, which were converted aircraft hangars standing side by side. One evening after the performance I was called from the officers' mess to adjudicate a pitched battle between the two groups. A map had been knifed, and the 'capa squad' was called to interpret when the combatants were separated at pistol point. It appeared that the difference of opinion had arisen from the ban on smoking in the theatre. The perks of dropped cigarette butts in the cinema were worth far more than the wages paid to civil labour. They were collected, dried, remade and repackaged to appear on the streets of Naples, looking almost as authentic as the black market brands on sale.

The local problem was settled by a new arrangement of day on, day off in theatre and cinema alternatively for our cleaners. The gift shop was stocked with cheap gewgaws from the thriving cottage industries of the Neapolitan back streets, and the troops dutifully purchased their small offerings to take home to wives and children they had not seen for months or years. There was a touch of pathos in the sight of tough, battle-hardened men leaving the premises clutching such improbable purchases as pink woolly animals and dolls. Some goods were posted home. Nuts, lemons and the like had not been seen in England for many years, and I am still saddened when I remember the reports of men later to die who had in good faith spent their meagre pay on small gifts for long-separated families only to have them stolen at the dockside in the UK before they fell into the hands of the GPO. The news to those of us who bore the main burden of the war, when dockers, miners or industrial workers went on go-slows or on strike for improvements in pay and conditions were more bitter than those in reserved occupations were aware of. The same had happened in 1914-18, when the dissociation of the front-line men was perhaps even more deeply felt and they had found the world at home strangely alien on their return on leave from the Western Front. Even those of us who returned to the universities after the war to find contemporaries who had read sciences now well into their doctorates found them strangely immature. We soldiers had grown up more quickly.

As the rains of the Mediterranean winter began to give way to spring weather in 1945 and the armies of the Allies started to knock at the door of the Third Reich, it became clear to us that the war would soon be over. Many Allied troops passed through our camp, now completed, and none caused more problems in transit than the Canadians. Exercise Goldflake involved us in handling a complete Canadian division and our resources were stretched to the limit. Of all the polyglot forces in Italy the backwoodsmen of French Canada were among the most volatile.

On one particular occasion the camp with its sentries and barbed wire perimeter constructed to keep the Italians out and our own men in was heavily patrolled and guarded. Large scale troop movements were high-security affairs even at this stage of the war, and the ten thousand or more Canadians in our camp were given orders that on no account might they leave the enclosure during the nights of transit. Such restrictions after a period of active service were undoubtedly unpopular and the whores of Naples were not far away. Most of these ladies who patrolled the galleria Umberto and the off limit areas of the town were in heavy demand, and from time to time VD was reported among transit troops. In the Canadian Army, as indeed in other Allied formations, it was an offence to contract VD. There could be few more pleasurably self-inflicted wounds that could keep a man out of battle. For this reason the armies provided PA (Prophylactic Aid) Centres, often in public lavatories requisitioned for the purpose by the town mayors. At such centres treatment was self-administered and a man's name recorded in the good book. Recourse to these records could, if claimed, exonerate a soldier who had clearly taken care to ensure that his night out did not have unfortunate consequences. Nevertheless, the VD rate was high at times and gave cause for considerable concern.

Our gallant Canadians were consequently required to remain in camp and for security reasons forbidden to visit the expert and accommodating ladies of Naples. On the morning after their stay as welfare officer, I was called upon by Jock Murray, our Scottish Medical Officer. During the previous night I had been on duty as orderly officer and had made the usual regular night visits to the sentries, turned out the guard twice as prescribed by military regulations and seen or had reported to me nothing untoward.

'There's going to be a hell of a security row about this' said Jock, handing me the Prophylactic Aid Centre register. Recorded within it were page after page of names of the licentious Canadian soldiers. Nearly a thousand of them had, somehow or other, got through the wire at night and visited the ladies of the town. But we heard no more of it. Lust will find a way and a few rolls of triple Danert wire were unlikely to deter our determined Canadian allies.

Later, after the war finished and I had taken up residence in Milan, I was to have a batman who was less careful. He was a devout Roman Catholic and had leave to go to a retreat from time to time at weekends organised by the padre. Between retreats he had a few spells in hospital for VD cures and I could not help envy him the simple rhythm of his moral philosophy, which provided a happy sequence of pleasure and penitence.

As the spring of 1945 began to bring the first signs of heat to southern Italy, the war moved towards its close. The armies had broken out into the plain of Lombardy and later moved up into Austria. The German armies surrendered and the Commander-in-Chief decreed that all ranks be given a day's leave on VE (Victory in Europe) Day. Jock Murray and I prepared the unit ambulance and spent the evening hours driving along the roads around the camp rescuing some of our inebriate soldiery. A great deal of local vino was drunk and there was a record sick parade the following morning.

Soon afterwards came news that I was to be posted to a new job. The Army Welfare Service had now, with the end of the war, temporarily acquired considerable importance. The Allied armies no longer had a foe in Europe, but the war in the Far East continued and the atom bomb had not yet been used. Many of us expected to be transferred to that theatre, but in the meantime there were huge problems in Europe. The war damage had been colossal. Refugees and displaced persons moved, often aimlessly, across the continent. The political settlement of Yalta had not crystallised into the iron frontiers of the Cold War and millions of allied soldiers, many of whom had been away from home for years, could think of nothing other than leave and loved ones. It was a time of ferment.

I was not to know that before the end of that year, at the age of 22, I would have command as a captain of the Army Welfare Services for Milan, Turin and Genoa. I was given a three-ton lorry and a driver and we set off northwards for Milan to what was to be an extraordinary responsibility at such a youthful age.

CHAPTER FIVE

ON LEAVE WITH THE ALLIES

War, for the front line soldier, is compounded of lengthy periods of boredom punctuated by short spells of fear. Tedium laced with terror is a heady cocktail, so it was as well that there were periods of leave when we could live it up in the cities of wartime Italy. It was here too that the men of many nations were to rub shoulders with one another as British, Americans, Poles, Portuguese, Free French, South Africans, Indian troops and many others of the now polyglot armies in Italy met and competed, when they were on the town, enjoying a few days away from their units.

Until Cassino was taken, the Via Roma in Naples was the axis along which the British squaddies and the American buck privates spent many of their off-duty hours. In the spring of 1994 this famous promenade, which leads from the Neapolitan waterfront into the heart of the city, was thronged with Allied troops. The shops did a roaring trade selling gifts, cheapjack ornaments and souvenirs, leather goods, sweetmeats of dubious origin, black market cigarettes, liquor or fruit, whilst in the flanking alleyways, marked off limits to Allied troops and guarded by the Military Police of both armies, were to be obtained the more urgent needs of the flesh. Along this *paseo* wandered the Allied soldiery in the hot sunshine. There were Americans in their well-pressed uniform, their officers in their 'pinks', British soldiers in shirt sleeve order, and reinforcements just arrived from UK still wearing the unbecoming long shorts which looked like the Indian Army rig of 1914-18.

There was little traffic except for a great variety of army vehicles – three-ton lorries, heavier American trucks with the white star of the 5th Army and British 30 cwt or 15 cwt runabouts. Amongst all this, frequently bringing the traffic to a halt, were the ubiquitous horse-drawn taxis which plied for hire in the various squares or on the waterfront.

When leave was granted and a pass had been obtained, the next problem was that of getting to the local Eldorado. Only the more senior officers had call upon their own transport. Junior officers and other ranks made use of their thumbs. This worked very well. It was almost mandatory for a service vehicle on the highway to stop and pick up members of the Allied forces who requested a lift. In places the roads were in a state of poor repair and shell holes had been filled in with loose material. But apart from one hairy journey with an American negro in a staff car at speeds of over 100 mph, I cannot ever recall feeling in great danger.

The major ports of call for most officers on arriving in Naples for leave were the British Officers' Club near the seaward end of the Via Roma and the American Officers' Club, known as the Orange Grove, and more airily situated on the hillside at the end of the main waterfront. The British Officers' Club served a meal of sorts, and it was possible to buy appalling bottles of Marsala and Lacrima Christi to wash it down. During the years of the occupation the Italians must have disposed of most of their undrinkable vintages through this substantial outlet. Nowadays the Mafia process it from chemicals. It was a fairly normal practice to lunch here, and then as the heat of the day built up to spend the afternoon with our American friends at the Orange Grove, where luxuries such as ice cream were on the menu. It was the practice in my unit to wear shirt sleeve order and khaki drill slacks with a Sam Browne. As a subaltern of twenty-two summers I looked at least eighteen years of age and on one occasion I hitched a lift with a brand new American, recently arrived in Italy in an equally brand new Jeep, up to the American Club. I was waiting at the bottom of the funicular when he screamed to a halt, jumped out of his Jeep, stood to attention and saluted. I asked if he was going to the Orange Grove. 'Yes sir!' he said. We whizzed up the hill and he jumped out, held the door open for me and threw a tremendous salute. I thanked him and he remained to attention as I walked away, gazing at my two pips.

'Any time, General', he said respectfully. I wondered who was kidding who, but I was fairly convinced from his respectful demeanour that he thought he had assisted a very juvenile two-star general of the British Army.

After a peaceful afternoon beneath the orange trees, it was usual to return to town. Choices of entertainment were limited and to some degree polarised between the highbrow option of the San Carlo opera and the lower brow dives beneath the arches of the Galleria Umberto. I tasted both. On one occasion I had struck up an acquaintance with an Italian cellist by the name of Alphonso Laudiro, who gave me a claque ticket (to bring in supporters) for Aida. Unfortunately the seat was so near to the orchestra that I could hardly see the stage, and I could certainly hear very little but Alphonso playing his cello.

Another evening proved to be rather more exciting. I had met a naval captain in the British Officers' Club and after a few drinks we repaired to a night club in a cellar underneath the floors of the Galleria. The place was full of ladies of the town, and we were entertained by a lively cabaret. What seemed to me to be large sums of money were being spent. Subalterns were allowed to draw 1200 lire a month of their pay, which was only three pounds, but as the more usual currency was cigarettes most of us got by and the rest of our pay was credited at home. Even so, the basic pay at that time was only thirteen shillings a day plus field and marriage allowance, which brought it up to about a pound.

Amongst the mixed clientele of the night club - reserved for Allied officers - were many Americans and Brazilians. The local ladies clustered around the latter like wasps around a honeypot. The Brazilians, who had recently joined us, were the highest paid and least effective troops in Italy, but they were generous in their tips to the hostesses.

After a while we were joined by some Americans, who proceeded to get very drunk and decided to express their confidence in their skill with firearms. We cast some doubt upon their abilities, and to our consternation some bottles were set up at the end of the bar, one end of the cellar was cleared and our new friends produced their revolvers. Shooting started, and the ladies rapidly disappeared. Ricochets whistled round the walls of the cellar and my naval friend and I beat a hasty retreat. As we left the Military Police arrived, so we thought it best not to stay for the last roundup.

The Americans never failed to surprise. I recalled a time in Northampton, my home town, and the arrival of Texan troops earlier in the war. The local branch of the National Provincial

Bank was located at the town centre in the Drapery, and the Texans, in their Jeeps were sent to collect money for their first pay parade. To the astonishment of the good burghers of that then sleepy market town, the Yanks roared in, tyres screaming and armed to the teeth with machine guns and revolvers. Two men jumped out and stood guard at the door of the bank. An officer was escorted in to collect the unit pay by two others, who then backed out with him covering the customers, apparently in case anyone should try a snatch. It was all very theatrical. They jumped back into their Jeep and roared off to their base, leaving behind an astonished audience.

Recently I was watching the film *Anzio*, which bore little if any resemblance to the realities of the Italian campaign. But the volatility and unpredictability of the American army which it reflected had an element of truth. There were substantial numbers of American servicemen of Italian origins, and after the landings in Sicily many family ties with the Mafia were recemented. The result of this, allied to the ease with which the quartermasters could write off stores and the generous provision of the PX (the American NAAFI), was bound to lead to a well-established black market and a deal of corruption, of which more in the next chapter.

One of the few advantages British officers had was access to a monthly ration of whisky. With several bottles you could buy a Jeep; in fact the price of one on the Anzio beachhead at one time was reliably reported as a single bottle. As a result of this we acquired some interesting ancillary equipment. Even in my Liverpool days I was able to borrow, on no more than a signature and an indefinite loan from an American unit stationed on the Grand National Course at Aintree, a .50 Browning machine gun, a formidable weapon, which we retained.

On the darker side our Allies could at times be a positive menace. Once, waiting for a truck in a Naples back street late at night to return to the unit, I was for no very clear reason held up and threatened at revolver point by a drunken American with his finger on the trigger. After a very uncomfortable few minutes the unit truck drew up and to my great relief he fled into the night.

In spite of encounters of this sort, the Americans brought an openness of mind and a vigour to the theatres of war of a tired Europe which was like a breath of fresh air. This breeze was both welcome and invigorating to those of us in the 8th Army who had long felt the burden of the war, of rationing at home and the blitz of the early years. The American's sheer mobility, their determination not to be deterred by physical obstacles and at their best a wider breadth of vision, extended our parochial European minds. As in 1918 at the end of the First World War, it brought us, at earlier stage this time, an injection of new blood. We made good friends of many of them and rapidly accepted and recognised each others' strengths and deficiencies.

It is not possible to generalise about the relations between our own troops and the local Italian population. These varied enormously. There are few more volatile people in Europe than the Italians, and few more phlegmatic than the British. When the language problem was added to this, the mixture which resulted was like that of oil and water. The two cultures rarely dissolved into solution except in bed, and much depended upon local circumstances.

Money also talked, and in my next chapter I will have something to say of the corruption of the black market. On the other hand, I can remember a brave priest running from cover to cover to give succour to the wounded under enemy fire and observation in full daylight during the Gothic line offensive when 46th Division was advancing on Trarivi, when he could have remained in safety within the walls of his church.

I recall, too the kindness of an Italian family in a small village near Lake Trasimeno when I went to visit the rough temporary grave of my only cousin, an artilleryman, who had recently been killed. They gathered flowers from the hillside and the village children accompanied me to the olive grove in which he had found a first resting place before reinterment by the War Graves Commission. They stood beside his grave and joined me in my tears.

The excitability of the Latin temperament was another matter. One evening, resting behind the lines in a small village, we watched the people of the hamlet streaming home from church along the rough main street after evening service. Two families, men, women and children, appeared to be avoiding one another and walked on opposite sides of the road in their Sunday best. The women were in black and the men in their only suits, badly cut and looking like Chicago reach-me-downs from the 1920s.

Suddenly one of the men shouted a volley of abuse which began with a robust 'porca Madonna' and finished with the unacceptable and derogatory 'disgrazia te'. A fight started between two men. This we could understand and accept. Next, bricks and stones started to fly. Then the women and children joined in. The women grabbed one another by the hair and within a few minutes of leaving the quiet of the evening service, there was a full scale fight in which all were involved and blood began to flow.

The British soldiery, uninvolved, stood aside and cheered the contestants on. But as the fracas dissolved into shouting and abuse, I could not but think of my peaceful village of Wootton in Northamptonshire, and the impossibility of anything like this after evensong at St George's!

After the capture of Cassino and the break out from the bridgehead at Anzio, the line moved onward to the north of Rome, and for a while warfare became more mobile, until the Tedeschi settled down into their Todt-built Gothic line. I had a couple of days' leave in Rome and attended a papal audience given for Allied officers, which involved a surprisingly personal visitation by the Pontiff. The Romans in their open city greeted us with open arms.

CHAPTER SIX

THE BLACK MARKET

I am sure there must be many better qualified than me to tell the story of the *borsanera* (black market) in wartime Italy. I was very young and very junior in rank, but in spite of this I touched the fringes of its dirty cloak on more than one occasion. Many senior officers must have had a wider perspective of experience. The exchange rate of the Italian lira in 1944 was 400 to the pound sterling. The pay of infantry subaltern was 13 shillings or 260 lire a day and we were allowed to draw 1,200 lire a month from our army pay, although it was rumoured that if need pressed you could get a bigger advance. £3 a month or 1,200 lire was not a fortune, even for a night out on the town in Naples.

The army was, however, in control of resources other than money. In particular, it had cigarettes. Whenever two economies co-exist side by side, one in surplus and the other in shortage, a black market will arise. The army had such a surplus, or at least one could say it had a source, even if such a source was not always in surplus. It had, as I have said, cigarettes. It also had petrol, food, clothing, spirits, medical supplies, tyres, weapons and vehicles. All these were in short supply. The Italians, on the other hand, had commodities which the army could not provide. These included, in particular, lire, which could purchase many of the delectable commodities which the British and American soldier had not seen since 1939. But above all, sex was for sale.

It had not been the policy of the War Office to provide the soldier with camp followers. Such things had been officially frowned upon since the new armies of 1916 had landed in France, and in any case Field Marshal Montgomery would not have approved in North Africa. But the imbalances between the two economies, military and civil, in southern Italy soon put all this right. The laws of supply and demand reasserted themselves and a thriving black market in which liquor, sex and tobacco were the principal currencies was soon to develop. It became increasingly refined as the war proceeded.

Life is the greatest education of all, and a boy brought up in a country village who had attended his local grammar school, had a year at the university and whose nose had been in books and feet in rugby boots, had little sophistication and knowledge of the ways of the world. Thirty years on, as I look at my war diary and my letters home, I realise how much we were innocents abroad. Even the youthful *scugnezzi* - the street boys of Naples - must have found us naive. The picture of the big, bad wicked world which unfolded before our youthful eyes was astonishing. It fell to my lot at various periods, both when I was with my regiment and later after leaving an officers' convalescent home, to brush up against this underworld of the *borsanera*, which had, for the Italians in particular, become a normal way of life.

My first serious encounter with the war within the war was not first hand. Antony Franklin and I had, after a period at the Infantry Reinforcement Depot (recounted in Chapter 8), reached the point when we could expect to join our regiments in the line. One evening there came an urgent message from the military police in the local area to load, at once, a Bren gun carrier (a lightly-armoured tracked vehicle) and proceed to a crossroads not far from Montesarchio where shots had been fired at a military police road block and a man wounded. It appeared that a group of deserters from the Allied forces, American and British, had for some time had in their possession three-ton lorries and a 15 cwt truck, and with two despatch outriders on motor bicycles they had been running grain and olive oil across the country. The Italians had no transport. Just as in nature life always fills and profits from any possible gap and cranny, this particular opportunity had not been neglected. Further, there were amongst the American forces a number of men whose family roots lay in Southern Italy, and darkly, it was said, in the Sicilian Mafia. What appeared even more incredible was that the group operating this particular enterprise included within it one or two German deserters.

There was certainly no doubt that the small convoy had failed to stop at a checkpoint and that shots had been fired. There was a hasty discussion by those in authority as to which victim to choose, and my old friend Antony was assigned to the task. Tony set off with his vehicles in the direction indicated by the military police, armed to the teeth with all the necessary appurtenances of a small guerrilla war. The road said to have been taken by the gang from the crossroads led up into the Apennines, and as night fell, high up and some way from the track into which it degenerated, they saw a fire burning.

They decided upon that invaluable element in war, surprise, as their best means of effecting an arrest. They parked their vehicles and the small platoon, led by my gallant friend, made their way through the olive groves in the gathering dusk, up the walled terraces of the hillside. After a climb of some hundreds of feet they found themselves on a crest overlooking a valley in which there were parked, in laager, a number of vehicles. In the best infantry manner the Bren guns were deployed to cover the riflemen, who moved forward. At a pre-arranged signal a burst was fired in the air over the heads of the small group around the fire and Tony called upon them to lie down and surrender. Having ordered their quarry to remain on the ground, the rifle section went forward to disarm them. There was an enraged cry from one of the spreadeagled fires. It took only a few minutes for my discomfited friend to find that he had disturbed a small mountain warfare school which was settling down for the night. Of the bandits there was no further news. No doubt they continued on with their profitable business whilst Tony and I prepared to face a sterner foe.

More often than not, however, the army was the victim of our predatory Italian friends and motor vehicles were in the habit of disappearing unexpectedly in spite of all the precautions. Shortly after the abortive pursuit of the gang of deserters, a neighbouring unit, resting out of battle behind the lines, decided to take matters into their own hands after losing very substantial quantities of stores and equipment in a series of well-organised thefts. The Commanding Officer decided to mount a raid on the nearby village in the early hours of Sunday morning, when the population would be sleeping off the Saturday night vino before attending Mass.

Each road leading into the central square was entered at first light by a heavily-armed patrol, and the inhabitants of houses and farms were brought from their beds by the knock of a rifle butt on the heavy doors. Haystacks, granaries, storerooms and other likely places were searched. The results were astonishing. We found complete motor vehicles stripped down to components, including a Jeep and a three-ton lorry, weapons - German as well as British - ammunition and a substantial variety of military impedimenta were uncovered and stacked in the village square. There was even the damning evidence of the adjutant's own canvas bath stamped with his name.

There was a great deal of commotion. The volatile Latin temperament of the Italian who has been deprived of property, however dubiously acquired, led to some heated exchanges. Tears flowed, hands were gesticulated and voices shrilled.

As the heap of booty grew in the square, the mayor was sent for. Small, dark and breathing garlic through his gold-filled teeth, he spoke eloquently of the great cost expended by his friends in purchasing quite legally most of the commodities displayed.

Back came the rejoinder from the Colonel. Possession of British Army property was an offence. No doubt the recently departed Tedeschi would have shot hostages, but the British were merciful. They would merely impound the goods which were rightly theirs. Everything was confiscated, but there were some who could not help feeling that our former foe might have had a rather rough deal. After that affair it became more difficult to get the laundry done for the traditional bribe of a bar of soap.

The theft of British and American army equipment throughout the campaign was substantial. There was one occasion on which a complete railway train was said to have disappeared. One method employed was to rob army lorries en route. A vehicle would slow down at a road junction and after arrival at its destination it would be found that stores had been thrown out by a stowaway who had jumped aboard unnoticed at the rear. It was not unknown for a substantial sum of money to change hands as a bribe for a vehicle to be stopped twice at two pre-arranged points.

As a result the army had to post an armed guard in any three-tonner conveying stores. There was, nevertheless, a fair amount of 'flogging' of army property by the servicemen. American quartermastering was less rigidly controlled than our own.

Cigarettes were always in demand. Soldiers received 50 free a week in tins, and after that more could be had at fourpence for 20. They could be sent from home at similar preferential rates. On the black market a packet would be worth up to 200 lire. Bully beef had a high exchange rate, and army blankets disappeared with great regularity. The Canadian forces, in particular, had an issue of high quality soft green blankets, and as winter approached the *haute couture* of Rome began to turn out well-cut overcoats in that unmistakable green blanket cloth.

These encounters between the civilian operator and the British soldier were usually a battle of wits, not always won by the local wide boys. Our cooks, who brewed the strong army tea as we moved north, would often do a fine trade with the locals. Having carefully stored the used tea leaves, they would wait until the unit was about to move. The leaves would be dried in the hot Italian sunshine and carefully repackaged in their original containers. A bulk sale would be made just before we left, through the channels that always seemed to be established whenever a unit had remained in one place even for a few days. I always wondered whether the Italians thought the British addicted to particularly weak tea, as I gathered there were few complaints from the customers. I suppose we could have claimed that our former foes were fair game for such tricks as these, but the army had cause to feel sore when gifts home disappeared. Unhappily, small purchases by soldiers of lemons or nuts sent back through the army post office were often rifled.

One regrettable but probably well-based suspicion was that the vultures lurked on the waterfront back at home. Some of our poorly-paid other ranks had been sent to Liverpool docks the previous year to unload cargoes of oranges. It had been rumoured that ships from Spain had had bombs placed aboard and the well-paid dockland fraternity had refused to touch the cargoes.

Our views about the toiling masses in reserved occupations at home were not always complimentary, but the Second World War was a total war in which the civilian population was deeply involved, and there was little if any of the strength of feeling that ran through the army in 1914-18 about war profiteers. Service to the nation was felt to have been more fairly apportioned. Neither did we have home leave from the battlefronts, which meant that men were away from any close contact with home for the duration. The realities of conflict, especially in the fighting units, were our main preoccupation, and we were only too well aware of the dangers civilians faced in the cities at home.

After leaving the front I was stricken with jaundice. On recovery I visited Army Force Headquarters at Caserta and was offered a job in Allied Military Government (AMGOT) until I was fit to return to the line. But enteritis intervened, and I was unable to do so. It was, however, while I was at AFHQ that I heard from senior officers in the mess of the concern felt about the activities of the 5th Army in Sicily, which was, of course

American and had been staffed with a number of men who had close family connections with the local Italian population. The Mafia had, as a result of repressive fascist administration, become substantially weakened. This was one of the few welcome by-products of Mussolini's reign. It had been decided by the American authorities that despite the criminal backgrounds of these people the balance of advantage lay with their being granted a measure of responsibility as liaison officers to establish civil administration in the occupied parts of southern Italy. The consequences of this for the post-war period were to prove very serious, for that decision helped the Mafia to become re-established in the south.

While this was to have repercussions for Italy long after the war, the activities of our own troops on the black market resulted in not a little profit for some of the more astute business minds in the 8th Army.

Most enterprising of all, however, was a member of the Jewish brigade who made a killing that was to be the talk of the army for weeks. On leave in Naples he wandered around the many shops along the Via Roma which sold cheap, gimcrack goods to the soldiers. Here he got into conversation with one of the proprietors. Amongst the most marketable commodities were base metal-cast cigarette lighters in the shape of gondolas, models of Vesuvius and other moulds of local or Italian significance. The shopkeeper explained how difficult it was for him to get supplies, as the lighters, which were a most saleable souvenir for the troops, would not work without flints. The imported flints were not available for the duration, and much trade of a most lucrative nature was being lost to the winds. Neither could the customers be persuaded to buy lighters without flints.

A letter was despatched home and the young Jewish corporal was glad to receive by an early post from the UK a large box. It contained a vast quantity of cigarette lighter flints, said to number more than a million. There followed a period of bargaining, and eventually a wholesale price was fixed of 9d per flint. The problem, however, of getting the profit of nearly £40,000 in lire home proved too much for the corporal, and rumour had it that he spent the rest of the war in great affluence sitting uneasily on a kitbag full of notes, which at times proved a great embarrassment to him.

The Via Roma of 1944 was the retail centre of the throbbing heart of the Neapolitan black market. On each side of the street between the busy shops were steep steps that led into the back alleyways, clearly marked off-limits, where sex was on sale to Allied troops. Nothing is more attractive than a place which is said to be out of bounds. At the entrances to these European kasbahs stood small boys, often no more than ten years old, shouting their wares. 'You wanna my sister, Johnny?' 'You wanna egganchips?' 'You wanna bigga beefsteak and fukka my sister?' On the walls adjoining were frequent plaques extolling the qualifications of numerous *dottore* who specialised in the cure of venereal diseases for the civilian population. The army also had its own prophylactic aid stations.

The American soldiers seemed to be much more licentious than the British. Perhaps they were better fed. They were certainly better paid. Nevertheless they seemed to be much more frequently approached by the *scugnezzi*. The astonishing thing, however, was that they were actually bought and sold. The youthful pimps would make the first contact with a promise of pneumatic bliss and the GI, often full of cheap marsala or Lacrima Christi from the many bars, would stagger off with his small keeper into the off-limit areas. Here he would, for a few cigarettes, be handed over to a more sinister gentleman and disappear into the warren of back alleys to what he hoped would be an amorous assignation. If he was reasonably sober with a companion in arms, there was a fair chance that the worst that would befall him would be ten days on a VD cure, if he forgot to register and get prophylactic aid. But if he was alone and drunk and darkness fell, he would often be found next day by the military police stripped of everything worth taking, including his boots. Sometimes he had passed through two or three hands as he was 'sold' up the line to the tougher operators.

After the war in Europe ended I was to move to Milan, where the black market was just as rife but where the manipulators were, if anything, more sophisticated. I was by now 23 years of age and having been promoted to a captaincy, I was to run army welfare services in Milan, Turin and Genoa. It was here that I ran into a quite extraordinary affair of illicit trading, one which took my breath away. The war in Europe was over and there were desperate shortages of food, which became more apparent each day. The German army had lived off the land in the closing stages of hostilities and the civilian population was desperately ill-fed. Major Edney, my CO, had departed on leave after many years in the Middle East to the UK and the No 2 army welfare service centre in Milan, with branches at Turin and Genoa, was left in my charge.

At about this time, late in 1945, a message came through from home to say that I was due for an early release as an exhibitioner of my college at Oxford, and that I would shortly be offered my discharge so that I would be able to return for the Lent term. On the same day, the Sergeant Major came to see me and asked for a private word in my ear. He was, he said, worried about our Ration Corporal. The latter was responsible for going to the bulk stores twice weekly to collect the unit's rations in a 15 cwt truck. According to the Sergeant Major, he had been drinking heavily and was making boasts in his cups about his financial standing that could hardly be ignored. He had been loading onto his vehicle, with the connivance of one of the storemen, an extra hundredweight each of sugar at the stores. This, of course, was almost worth its weight in gold to the sugar-starved civilians of Milan. But the transaction that followed was less straightforward than expected. His next call was a farm in the Gorgonzola area, where he exchanged his sack of sugar for cheeses. These he then carried to Milan, hidden in the vehicle, to be sold to another contact in the city. He was now in possession of substantial sums of lire. He then proceeded to a branch of the Banca di Napoli, where a friendly bank clerk who was receiving a *douceur* exchanged the lire for sterling.

Our friend was in the habit of sending home to his wife, through the post, parcels of dirty washing on the overland route which had now reopened across Europe with the end of the war. In the socks were bundles of notes. He had claimed, in his drinking bouts, that he had so far got £7,000 home in this way, which at today's value of sterling represents a sum of over £200,000.

I must admit that I was staggered at the scale of this operation, although I am sure it must have been chickenfeed in comparison with some of the black market activities which were commonplace in wartime Europe. I consequently telephoned the Provost Marshall's office to ask for advice. To my astonishment I was told that they had far bigger fish to fry and if I intended to do anything about it I had better get on with the job myself. Accordingly I detailed an NCO who I thought I could trust to tail the ration corporal on his next visits to the stores, but we drew a complete blank.

After checking several of his journeys, I sent for him at my office overlooking the Duomo in the main square. I thought it best to try bluff, and confronted him with the whole story, indicating that I knew everything and that he would be wise to spill the beans. I would then do all I could to see that he was treated reasonably, for he had been a good soldier. He turned white, and we spent a long time questioning him, but he never broke.

A few days later I left for home and eventually the Lent Term at Oxford, rationing and life on a scholarship income. I have every reason to believe that on his release shortly afterwards, my corporal started back in civilian life a fairly wealthy man by our standards of those days. I often wonder how he fared later. Today we are far more accustomed to hearing stories of great gain made by the criminal fraternity. It is difficult to return in our imagination to the past. to those days when the riding of a bicycle without lights or finding a purse and not handing it in to the police were regarded as serious matters. We were far more law abiding and law conscious in our youth in the 1930s, and the world was a better place for it. The war probably had a great deal to do with it, as in particular, it engendered a contempt for public property. The safety net of the welfare state, acceptable as it must be, has also proved to be a mesh which can strangle as well as save.

So it was that in the crucible of the sacrifice of war the metal of many was refined, but the slag too often came to the top. However, we left home as boys, but those of us who returned from the fighting units were men, if not men of the world.

CHAPTER SEVEN

TAKING STOCK

Much has been written about world wars by the field marshals, generals, the captains of men and the military historians. A young man in his late teens or very early twenties is not always aware that he is involved in great matters which are the fabric of history in the making, or of the significance of the affairs of the times through which he is living. It is only in retrospect that the pieces of the jigsaw fall into place and complete the puzzle which his own youth, and his own participation in the puzzle, made obscure.

Nor do I think that those of us who were still at school when the war began were as politically conscious as the youth of today. Rapid communication and the assault of the mass media upon our opinions were, as yet, in their infancy. Like so many of the young of those times, we saw the world in black and white with a naive simplicity and lacked an understanding of the events of the day in the context of history. So it was that our view of the Russian extension of power into central Europe had not fallen into the perspective which, with hindsight, we now recognise as one of the great movements in the international balance of power of our times. The emergence of the superpowers had only penetrated into our political subconscious, and we still saw the world through the rose-tinted spectacles of youth.

The attempted rape of Finland by the Soviets in the winter war of 1940, it is true, had worried many of our consciences, but the Spanish Civil War, Abyssinia and the Third Reich and the Nazis had been sufficient to make most of us uneasily grateful that the Russian bear was embracing the German eagle in a death struggle in the East. The chill wind of potential disaster which had blown from the Continent in 1940 was stilled. We were not alone in the fight against fascism, and this was enough.

Shortly before the assault of the 8th Army upon the defences of the Gothic line around Coriano on the Adriatic coast in the late summer of 1944, all the officers of 46 London Division were called together by Field Marshal Alexander in a cinema. He had, he told us, recently been to London and had seen the Prime Minister. In the meantime the army had done a good deal of work with decoy material to convince the enemy that our main attack might fall upon their Adriatic flank rather than in the west of the peninsula. But in spite of this, the 8th Army was still to attack on the Adriatic side. The purpose, said Alexander, was to get as far as possible into Austria before the Russians enveloped it.

There was an audible buzz at the meeting as we had our first introduction to post-war political realities. There has been much criticism since the war of Churchill's preoccupation with the Mediterranean campaign, almost as a vindication of a lost Gallipoli, but there can be no doubt of the rightness of his judgment in seeking to contain the Soviets as far east as might be practicable, so we set off to battle with new thoughts in our minds.

I was later to meet Russian officers at the officers' convalescent home at Trani. These were men who had been working with the Yugoslav forces and it was never possible to talk to them alone. There was always the inevitable companion, and although we played chess, any conversation which verged on the political resulted in a withdrawal of contact. I was to have the same experience after the war when visiting General John Sharp as his guest in the Rhine Army, where I met several of the Russian generals, each with his political shadow.

At Trani there were many children who had lost a foot or an arm working for the partisans across the other side of the Adriatic. I recall today Stalin's reaction when Churchill described to him the flail tanks and other devices for clearing minefields. One of these was the 'serpent', which I saw used. It involved firing a rocket to which was attached a 'snake' filled with amatol, later to be exploded as it lay across the minefield. It was most spectacular and quite effective. Stalin's prescription to Winston however was that marching infantry were the best way of finding mines, and indeed they were so used on the Russian front to trigger the mines and make way for the elite assault troops, who could tread in safety over their corpses. I have often wondered whether a nation gets the government or the leaders it deserves!

As a geographer I am convinced that in substantial degree the national temperament is a reflection of geography, and in particular of climate. The *dolce vita* was a far cry from the harsh climate of the heartland of the former Russian empire. But the Italian character was a different matter.

I had reason to reflect upon this when one bright day, convalescing at Sorrento in the autumn of 1944, we were taken by a group of those incomparable ladies, the Queen

Alexandra's Imperial Nursing Service, to visit one of Signor Mussolini's recently-vacated residences. This was an exquisite little house in a beautiful garden on a hillside on the Sorrentine peninsula. The day was hot, but the house was beautifully cool and the floor and walls were tiled to the ceiling. Here, we were told, the great dictator had repaired

with his mistress, Clara Petacci. While the rest of the party examined the lower floor of the premises I repaired upstairs with a well-endowed nursing sister to examine the more intimate quarters where, I guessed, the couple had spent much of their time. In Mussolini's bedroom was what I suppose we would call today a king-sized double bed. We sat down together on one side of it and admired the view through the window.

Suddenly there was a resounding crash. The bed fell apart and other members of the party soon joined us upstairs. As the officer who broke Mussolini's bed, my reputation was greatly enhanced!

Later I was to move north to Milan as the army entered the cities of northern Italy. When we arrived the bullet-riddled body of the Great Dictator had been strung up ignominiously by its heels from the roof of a petrol station, alongside his mistress.

I also met another lady, a beautiful, dark-haired, olive-skinned Roman, who claimed to be a former girlfriend of Field Marshal Kesselring. She was a member of a concert party which entertained our unit at Barra, near Naples, and I had the envied task as Welfare Officer of acting as her escort after the show. If indeed she was Kesselring's girlfriend as she claimed, I could not but admire his taste. The better class ladies of the town changed sides freely as the war moved up the peninsula, and the British and Americans were welcomed with very open arms!

Less fortunate were the refugees from the concentration camps and the many displaced persons who began to filter home as the war ended. I remember even now, to my shame, how badly I treated one neurotic girl who we employed towards the end of the war and who had been sent as forced labour to Germany. We were very young and very naive and almost disbelieving of the stories which filtered through at this time of turmoil about the concentration camps and their horrors. But at least our innocence and disbelief reflect the image of the British soldier as perhaps one of the best conquerors if one has to suffer an occupation as a vanquished country. Even the end of the war and the VE day celebrations were received phlegmatically by the army in Italy. Perhaps it was because we expected soon to receive marching orders for the Far East, for the Japanese enemy was still unbeaten. The British soldier was equally phlegmatic when the 'khaki election' of 1945 heralded changes which were to have profound results for our post-war society. The pamphleteers of the Army Bureau of Current Affairs did their best, many of us felt, with a bias to the left to interpret the political climate at home to the men serving abroad.

Soon after the end of the war in Europe I moved to Milan, and as I shall describe in the next chapter I became involved in army welfare. It was here that I had an urgent telephone call from Como asking for a loan of golf clubs and other articles for Churchill's party. The now deposed Prime Minister was licking his wounds after the election. When I met the officer who came to borrow the articles required, he described to me the sharp bitterness of Winston at what he felt to be, at the time, an utterly unexpected rejection by the electorate. In fact, there had been no slight. The old man was much loved by men of all political persuasions in the Army. Great men must make great decisions and make great mistakes. He had his share of all these. But we knew that his strength had held everything together in 1940 when he had expressed through his oratory the will and the resolve of the British people, and it was only later that the war was won by Russian manpower and American material. But for me the war was now over. The atom bomb had put the closure on our expected departure for the Pacific. Those who decry today the dropping of the bomb should try to extend their imagination to the understanding of the feelings of those who had at that time carried the burden of the long war; or perhaps they should talk to the survivors of the Japanese prison camps. So instead of a voyage to the Far East I left for Milan, and soon after that I returned home.

CHAPTER EIGHT

THE AFTERMATH OF WAR

We set up our headquarters near the Cathedral in the centre of Milan, in the Via St Andrea, in some well-appointed flats recently vacated by local *fascisti* and commandeered by the Army, whilst a few blocks away on the main square opposite the Duomo we occupied a suite of offices. The local swimming pool was amongst the many facilities which we reserved for the use of the army, and contacts were established with the dignitaries of the city.

Our first-floor flat had been stripped of furniture, including the cooker, and we installed our canvas beds and other camping impedimenta in fine rooms beneath high carved ceilings and candelabra. Lacking proper cooking facilities, we unpacked an army stove and knocked a hole through the roof to provide a flue. We employed an excellent cook, through the civil labour bureau, and with the aid of the occasional well-placed bottle of mess whisky began to enjoy food of a quality which we had not tasted since the war began.

As we sat down after an excellent dinner one day, Jack Murray, my batman, came running into the dining-room. 'Sir!' he shouted, 'the mess is on fire!'

'Don't be a fool, Murray', said Captain Grigg, the OC.

'But sir, we're on fire!' cried Murray.

So out we went and sure enough smoke was coming from the hole in the roof. The army stove pipe had heated the timbers and we were truly ablaze. We telephoned for the brigade and within minutes it arrived. The uniforms of the Italian fire service of those days looked like a cross between those of the comic opera and that of the general staff of a South American army. There was much shouting and excitement worthy of a Keystone Cops movie, but eventually the fire was brought under control.

We repaired later to our damp beds and thought no more of it. Under my pillow was my revolver. We were still infantry men and it was difficult to adjust to soft living with a roof overhead. Like all the young we were high-spirited and the war was over. From our office opposite the cathedral, from which we controlled the local theatre, cinema and other facilities requisitioned for the army, we blew up hundreds of French letters and distributed them into the breeze from the balcony onto the heads of the astonished local populace, whilst in a flat across the road from our quarters a lovely girl undressed each evening and we took it in turns to look at her with hungry eyes through our army binoculars.

After a time the OC was released from the Services and Captain Edney took his place. In turn he left for home, and in the late summer of 1944 I found myself in command with a third pip on my shoulder. Not long after, I had weekend leave and together with Pat Burton, another young captain, went off to Venice. We had been lent a palace on the Grand Canal by a local magnate and we set out in a Jeep, loaded with hard-boiled eggs and bottles of vermouth. This was our first leave for over a year, and we arrived safely only through good fortune. The war had been long and hard and we made the best of it, sleeping together in a four poster and doing the nightspots of the city. A later leave on Lake Como in the Villa Churchill at Cernobbio was equally exciting, with a day 'fishing' on the lake, once again with explosives and a crate of beer to drink.

In Milan itself the town was ours. We spent little of our pay, cigarettes were good enough currency, and we lived like kings. Pat Burton ran the swimming pool with the help of an Italian who claimed to be a close relative of Al Capone and, as I have described earlier in an account of the gorgonzola cheese racket, I could well believe it.

The black market was rife and life was easy. I was rather glad that we had won the war and that I had survived. But there was a strange unreality about it all. The Director of Army Welfare Services never came to visit us and we seemed to be answerable to no one. Over the course of a few months we lived the sort of life none of us had ever enjoyed before and few were likely to enjoy again for many years. The fruits of conquest were sweet and we savoured them to the full. But it was not to last. The dons had been busy back at Oxford, and on the same day I was offered an early release to continue with my degree course at the university, whilst the Army suggested I go north for the winter and run the Army Ski Hotel in the Alpine resorts. I chose the former. Towards the end of November I handed over my responsibilities and left Milan station for home.

The journey across war-torn Europe was long and tedious. The carriages had lost their window glass and viaducts were shaky, so we proceeded with caution. As we passed through neutral Switzerland, stopping at some of the stations, we were cheered by the populace. In France we were fed in marquees put up specially along the line, and here again we were cheered and applauded. Some of the local people wept when we stopped at unexpected halts. I remembered the weeping women on the streets of Liverpool on that grey morning of our departure a lifetime ago.

When we reached Dover, no one wept. England looked drab, the people tired and war-weary. We had won the war, but we had lost our youth and nothing would be the same again. There are periods in life when time seems to stand still and when the repetitive routine of life arrests the clock. But three years or more of war, for us, had brought with them an intensity of changing experience that made those early days at Oxford seem a lifetime away.

It was with thoughts like these that I was to return to the university in an ill-fitting demob suit a few weeks later. Clothes were still rationed and my service dress was being dyed to serve as a sports jacket. My old schoolfriend Ralph Hudson, now completing his doctorate, had spent the war taking part in the Chalk River project, which culminated in the explosion of the atomic bomb. He was now engaged in low temperature research at the Clarendon. John Prue, another schoolfriend later to profess in organic chemistry, was deep into research. But there was a generation gap between our contemporaries in years and ourselves. The war had placed what seemed to be an indelible print upon us for life. We seemed to have grown up far beyond our years.

Still younger than our own former school colleagues, who had not seen the active side of war, were those who now joined us from schools as undergraduates. We had, furthermore, a new urgency to work and to make up for lost time. It was commonplace for those who taught us to remark that we worked harder than any generation they could remember. We were more conscious of passing time and we knew more of life than our years admitted. Indeed, Bob Steele, my tutor for one term, seemed younger than myself.

Above all I found myself aware that I was living on borrowed time. Each day I could not but be astonished that I had survived. Beside this, smaller things no longer mattered. I worked hard for a good degree, was eventually vivaed for a first and came out near the top of the class list. But above all else was the heightened awareness of the life into which we had survived through the holocaust of the war. Food was in short supply and the bitter winter of 1946 with its coal shortages added a drabness to the life of the new socialist England.

Sir Frederick Ogilvie, now Principal of the college, entertained us kindly from time to time in the lodgings with Lady Ogilvie and we talked to him of the war. At one such party I spent much time one evening in conversation with a bright young former don, and not knowing his identity, I criticised vehemently the government of the day under Clement Attlee. I told him that I did not think it was the world for which we had fought the long war. Eventually he introduced himself. His name was Harold Wilson, then Minister of Works in the post-war Labour government.

But it had been a justified war. As the realities of all that had happened in Central Europe were revealed, we began to understand that we had done a job that had had to be done. My old tutor, J N L Baker, then Reader in Historical Geography, had long arguments with me about the shape of post-war Europe. Through the eyes of youth and with the experience of war, we could see no other way but that Europe should unite. But the older generation was too much with the past, and neither those at Westminster nor those in the groves of academe could believe that this must be so.

To some degree, we felt not so much betrayed but simply that no one would listen to us. This was a message we must all heed. Youth sees the world with new eyes and often has much to say, and age should listen. As the rate of change in the world quickens, this is of supreme importance. Youth now has a repository of wisdom of the world and an ability to interpret it to age, and more so than it has ever had in the past. They are the first generation to live in a world in which no one has lived before.

In one other respect we belonged to a generation which had had another peculiarly formative experience. The war had taught us the importance of self discipline. However, the constraints of life in college did not seem so attractive and although most of us were offered rooms we elected to live out in digs.

Quite by chance I met my old friend Graham Midgeley, later to be Dean and Vice Principal of St Edmund Hall. Together with Gerald Nation-Tellery, war wounded and a nephew of the Grand Duchess of Bavaria, we set up in digs in Headington. One evening, as three old soldiers, we were drinking quietly at the White Horse Inn on Headington Hill. Mr Buckle, the landlord, who we knew well, came into the bar to tell us that the proctors were outside. He hid us in the ladies' lavatory and we escaped a fine. On another occasion I was visiting Trevor Philpott at Cambridge, an old schoolfriend now working for the BBC and living with Phil Goodhart, then the MP for Beckenham. Once again, as ex-servicemen we were enjoying a quiet pint when the proctors came to ask why we were not wearing our gowns. I was able to tell them that I belonged to the other university. But I wonder what the reaction of young people of 25 would be today, had they fought through a major war, if they were to be asked about their business by the university police in this manner?

We had been men under discipline and accepted that these were the rules made by those in authority which we must obey. We did not question them and accepted our punishment accordingly. We then in our turn took charge of the affairs of the world, at the top of our profession and often responsible for great enterprises. However we were then asked to involve everyone, down to the cleaners, in the administration of our affairs! Wryly I cannot help feeling that we have lived the wrong way round. Subject to authority and unquestioning obedience in our youth, we in our turn must now consult everyone ad nauseam. We are in our turn at the beck and call of them all, from union officials to health and safety at work busybodies. Indeed, if our generation had been obsessed by health and safety we would not be living in the sort of society we now enjoy.

A few decades ago I decided that the time had come to return to the battlefield. With friends I rented a farmhouse in Tuscany and one morning set off across the Apennines towards the east coast and the battlefields of that long-ago winter war of 1944. As we approached the high hills behind Rimini, names like Coriano, Gemmano, Montescudo, Monte Colombo and Trarivi began to appear on the signposts. I made my way into Monte Colombo up a steep hill to the church where we had sheltered from heavy shellfire, and then to a sunny bar in the main street. 'Yes!' said the locals. They remembered those days of battle. Beyond the main street was a rough track along which I had led my platoon. At the end of it, to my astonishment, there still stood the ruined farm in which Sergeant Mansfield had been seriously wounded as he stood beside me with the 0 group and where Lieutenant Jones and a corporal had been killed beside me. The ground fell away to Trarivi and the picture which had been blotted out as the building collapsed around us in that far-off day in 1944 was recreated.

We walked silently back to the car. Thirty years vanished and became moments. When you have been granted a second life, it is strange to return to the place where you were born.

A car stopped and a voice asked in poor Italian if we were seeking something. It was a German returning to the battlefield upon the same mission. No, I did not know the way to the German cemetery, but he could tell me where the British one was at Gemmano. And so we drove on.

A small Italian girl followed us curiously as we walked from the car park to the cemetery. It had not been my first visit to one of these places, for I had already stood over my cousin's grave earlier in the holiday near to Trasimeno.

The rows of white stones were marshalled in the warm sunshine, row upon row on well-watered lawns. We checked the plan and I walked over to my platoon. Here they lay, the familiar names at the far side of that bridge of thirty years. We did not speak. It is difficult to speak through tears. I reflected upon their last days and the world that had since intervened, and wondered what they would have thought about it all if they could have returned. Age had not wearied them, nor had the years condemned.

Further north, in another cemetery, lay Tony Franklin, who had been my companion and friend at Oxford and through the war. I turned my back and went to the car park to live on some more borrowed time and ponder again upon the old lie *dulce et decorum est pro patria mori*. There are no generations. There are only experiences. Those whom we can most easily grasp by the hand, be it in time or space, are those who have shared common dangers with us.

As my friends lay before me in the warm Italian sunshine I could but reflect that we are their unfulfilled future and the burden upon us to ensure that we do our best to discharge our debt to their posterity. And so my thoughts went back to those days between the wars, with a vision of a classic cartoon of the 1920s when Clemenceau at the peace conference says to Lloyd George 'I thought I heard a child crying', while in the corner of the room lies an infant swaddled in a cloth on which is written 'class of 1920'. Those years when the seeds of yet another chapter in the European Civil War were to be sown by governments weakened in resolve by the losses of the best of their generation on the Somme and in other battles shaped our childhood in the twenties and thirties. They are, in effect, lost in transition in the context of our times today. The past is in truth another country, visited in reality only by those who have lived within it.

In the following chapters I will endeavour to put colour on the landscape of the lives we lived in those days when the shadows presaged the coming of a wider and yet more terrible conflict.

CHAPTER NINE

A VILLAGE CHILDHOOD

As Rousseau said, man is born free. Here there is a paradox, for physical chains swaddle us more closely in our infancy. Helpless, naked, the human animal's first exercise of the will is the demanding cry which summons the parents to find the necessary panacea to extinguish it and reestablish peace. The first few years are lost in the mists of trailing clouds of forgetfulness rather than those of glory, and it is beyond these that I attempt to trace the course of the yellow brick road which led from a small Northamptonshire village in the 1920s. Everything Dad did seemed to go wrong. Back from the 1914-18 war, an outfitter by trade, he had married a teacher called Flo, my mother, and their small savings had gone into a village store. The tiny income from the shop and mother's supply teaching had kept the four of us - my parents, my sister and I - for those first five infant years. Lofty and out of reach were the glass bottles of Jones' Crystal sweets. Nearer to hand and temptation were the tins of biscuits kept firmly closed at night against the mice that father tried from time to time unsuccessfully to dislodge from the premises. Sun faded picture postcards, newspaper racks, a tray of cakes, buttons, shoelaces. Goods on sale or return served to bolster the overheads of the essential stock in trade. It was a thin and precarious living, with a busy night on payday when the last week's debts were settled. Figures were anxiously added up in the back room against the end of the month, when the travellers' bills would come in for settlement.

As I said earlier, of all the senses, that of smell is probably the one which most readily evokes nostalgia. But hearing is perhaps the one which first impinges sufficiently indelibly to leave a first impression in the memory banks of the temporal lobes. And so it was that the clanking of the shunting wagons in the railway sidings of Woodford-cum-Membris has always been evocative of my days of infancy and perhaps the loss of innocence.

With Dad in the shop and on days when Mother had a supply teaching job, help had to be found. For a shilling a day a day a girl looked after my sister and me in a bare boarded room upstairs. Ada Radford, our first guardian, was an angel and we loved her dearly, but she soon left us for the big house in Byfield. The next incumbent lasted for but a short time.

By now I was learning to walk. Nancy's teaching technique was to stand, legs apart, while I clutched her knees beneath her skirts. I may have been dimly aware that more pleasant pastures lay beyond and Nancy seemed, as I dig into a subconscious recall, to enjoy the fumbling fingers of tiny hands. But mother walked in one day and did not approve, and Nancy soon left us. Woodford-cum-Membris indeed! And her successor soon showed her disapproval when I sought to improve further my toddling explorations in this pleasurable but unorthodox way.

The quality of education available at village schools in those days was very uneven. Resources were short and much depended upon the good luck of having a dedicated teacher.

Woodford-cum-Membris was not well endowed in this respect, and so when an opportunity arose for the purchase of a small general store at Weston Favell on the fringe of Northampton it was decided

that we should move and try our luck in a newly-developed estate on the edge of the town. A small house adjoined the shop, money was borrowed for a large mortgage and Dad, always optimistic and believing that prosperity lay around the corner, despatched my sister and me to a small private day school known as the Weston School of Music. At this establishment two elderly ladies taught nice children from the age of five French and the pianoforte, even dabbling at times in the three Rs. My earliest recollections include sitting at a piano stool after it had been occupied by a small girl and wondering why the seat was wet. She had apparently not enjoyed her lesson and I got the blame.

There were great excitements at the school when the misses Beazley announced that a new pupil was arriving - at least for music lessons. We were told her name was Lady Ann Spencer. We were not to know that her niece would one day step into the role of our future queen.

The school accordingly became very upmarket and the fees increased so that only those with silver spoons could afford them, in the twenties before the crash. But for us the silver plate was very thin. The depression came, bankruptcy followed and the house and shop were sold to meet the demands of creditors. The window which had been opened for two or three infant years onto a different world was now firmly closed. A deep darkness was to descend on the family, and it would be many years before I was to glimpse again, as an Oxford Exhibitioner, the daylight in which the middle classes bask.

Mother pawned her wedding ring. After all, it was Christmas. The receivers allowed us two beds, a table, chairs and personal possessions. Uncle Jack rented us a house in the downtown area with a nice view over the cemetery from which we could see our grandmother's grave. Dad, in the meantime, unsuccessfully sought work. Mother applied for teaching posts, but was told that it was not the policy of the town to employ married women as teachers. However, out of town the village schools were less particular, especially in the less salubrious parts of the county. Her name was taken and after a year she was informed that at the village of Wootton, where there was an old workhouse, a settlement of itinerant gypsies and later an army barracks, there was a temporary post for an infants' teacher.

By this time hunger was beginning to bite. Handouts for the unemployed were not as generous as they are today, and Uncle Jack's rent was more than we could manage. But another uncle lent us £25, to be repaid at the rate of ten shillings a week, to finance the cost of removal, and with hope in our hearts we moved out of town to the village, where the chairman of the school governors rented us a cottage at eighteen shillings a week. Mother accepted the job, which was later to become a permanency. The future seemed more secure and the shadow of the workhouse had receded.

The village school was like many of its kind in those days, but even so it was something of a shock at first. Two classrooms accommodated over a hundred children. The infants were with Mother in the smaller room, heated by a coal fire. In the larger room, the Headmaster presided over the eight to 14 year olds, assisted by a supplementary teacher who possessed, as I recollect, two passes in the School Certificate, in needlework and cookery. It had a tortoise stove in the middle. This room was occupied by about 80 children and the larger and more boisterous boys usually seemed to occupy the area in the vicinity of the sole source of heat.

At some later date the local authority deemed it wise to erect a screen across the room to separate the eight to 11 year olds from the 11 to 14 year olds. This was heralded in the inspector's report as 'the greatest single improvement in this village school since it opened'. I was to quote this many years later at the Department of Education and Science when I was planning a new grammar school in outer London, when open plan was the current ill-advised policy. But it helped me to get my way with the architects at the DES.

But more of that later. For the meantime, the screen was to ensure that we smaller children would be left to the mercy of the supplementary teacher, soon to become the village butcher's wife. Poor Mary had few powers of discipline with the unruly village boys. When the screen was drawn across after morning prayers the fun began.

So we had singing.

William Taylor was a brisk young sailor
He grew courting a lady fair
Bells were ringing, sailors singing
As to church they did repair.

It soon became apparent that Mary's paramour, the local butcher, was Eric Taylor, so his name was substituted and for 'sailor' we were singing 'butcher' The headmaster put matters right with the cane. But singing at least kept the sounds of misrule away from the ears of the Headmaster next door. After the dawn chorus, classes relapsed into chatter and indifference and I learned little or nothing of use. Later I was to reflect on how much I might have sown for future harvests if I had been at the Dragon School at Oxford, or some such other illustrious institution. But I learned a great deal about life outside the classroom. The school had a lobby for our coats, and outside across the yard, which was of dry dust or mud depending upon the season, were the girls' and boys' lavatories. It was reliably rumoured that if a boy went into the girls' lavatories he would at the very least spend the next few years doing hard labour at the local reformatory school at Tiffield, always a threat that hung over the heads of the unruly.

The nearest we ever got to the Mecca beyond the wall was by the proxy of aiming over it. This was an exciting and competitive sport. The more enterprising stopped at the village pump in Water Lane in order to tank up on the way to school. A nice judgement had to be made between taking in too little or too much. Too much meant a visit to the bogs before break time, a loss of pressure, audience and prestige and a weak showing against rival competitors. Nitty Reynolds was the acknowledged expert. By judicious squeezing of the member he could project well over the six foot wall. Some of the more forward girls applauded his efforts. We were all used to the farmyard. The open cubicles were less pleasant, especially at the end of the month when the lavender cart came round. No disinfectant was used in those days and you were lucky to find a few squares of newspaper on the seat.

But outside was the playground, and freedom. A circle was drawn in the dry dust on my first day. An opponent was selected of about the same weight and size. It was all very fair. Toby was a farm labourer's lad, well built and muscular. It was made clear that we had to wrestle.

Nothing like this had ever happened to me before, but I did not find the contest unpleasurable. As I recall, we were evenly matched and it ended inconclusively. But my acceptance into the tribe was now assured. Toby had leather knee pads. My knees were cut and the scabs were soon reinfected. But mother had some pads made for me and I became one of the boys. The future seemed assured, and after all I was better off than most. Although Dad was unemployed we had Mother's £4 per week, less the ten shillings paid back of Uncle Bert's loan of £25 and eighteen shillings a week rent. A farm labourer was paid 35 shillings a week in those days, so most of my friends wore at least some cast-offs from Dad or an elder brother.

Small boys wore boots several sizes too large which were shod with steel blakeys. These set up sparks if you slid on the flinty road surface and were the general footwear at every village school. Sometimes the boots had no laces, and if they were too large for the wearer fell off when we were playing High Cockalorum. This involved two teams, the leader of which bent down and rested his shoulders against the school wall. The rest of the team formed an elongated rugby scrum behind him and the other side then endeavoured to leapfrog over the line as far as possible to the wall. The game usually collapsed in the dust or mud. Oddly enough I was invited to play it again as a young headmaster in the RAF mess at Akrotiri in Cyprus together with the Headmaster of Emmanuel School, Charles Kuyper, and a number of other public school headmasters and vice-chancellors visiting the Air Force on a career jaunt.

At the village school, Stag (stag stag a roney, my black pony) was also played with vigour. Two boxes were marked out in the dust and from one to the other boys ran seeking to avoid being touched by a single guardian who operated in between the two safe havens. If he touched you, he took your hand and formed the beginning of a chain which progressively lengthened to guard the base. The hands at the end of the chain were the critical ones, for if they touched you you had to join the chain. Large and heavy boys were usually the winners, for they could break through the centre of the chain and regain the other base.

Meanwhile the girls played hopscotch in their part of the playground, which we were forbidden to enter under pain of unthinkable sanctions. Tip cat, five stones, hoops made of old iron wheel rings from the blacksmith with a wire hook to control them, whips and tops, marbles, conker fights and cigarette card competitions filled our playtime hours. None of these cost more than a few coppers. Most were home made.

Some of the more skilful boys became cigarette card barons. A card was placed against the wall and a line was drawn in the dust a few yards away. Turns were taken to flick a card at the target, holding the card between the first and second finger to get a good flighted spin. The one who first struck the target took the pool. In these days of sophisticated toys I cannot but wonder to what extent we are inhibiting the imagination of the young, who need to develop their own creativity. A bag of marbles and a few sheets of old graph paper kept me happy for many an hour creating mathematical games involving speed, distance and, colour by colour, competitive excitement. I was also the proud possessor of about half a dozen Dinky toys, which served the same purpose.

But all was not play. The school day began with prayers conducted by the Headmaster. This was followed by the learning of the Catechism, against the expected arrival of Canon Dodson, the Chairman of the School Governors, whose vicarage was across the road. My mother had never, apart from her wedding day, attended any place of worship, nor had my sister, and we had consequently received no overt religious instruction. Arriving at the village Church of England school was something of a new experience, and our first task was to catch up with the Catechism; I was not even sure what all this was about, but being an obedient child I applied myself loyally to the task. I was fortunate in possessing a great facility for learning by heart, even if the matter in hand was beyond immediate comprehension, and I can still recite most of the verse I learned in those early days.

The Catechism began 'What is your name?' After this came the reply in the printed book 'N or M'. As my name is Norman and that of my sister is Molly, I assumed that there must be a special edition of the work provided at great expense for each individual family. I soon caught up with the rest of the pupils, who had spent many years learning it by heart each morning, but there were some sections which troubled me in that they contained references with which I was not familiar. I had the temerity to put up my hand and enquire what was the meaning of the injunction forbidding adultery. I was informed by the Headmaster that this need not concern us, as it was quite clearly a crime committed only by adults and that no further questions were to be asked about it.

It was not long after this that I fell out with him. I was taking a childish interest in astronomy and had been to the public library, where I had done some reading about the subject. The sun, he reliably informed us, was the largest object in the universe. Up came the hand of young Galileo to contradict his authority and suggest that many of the stars were substantially larger. This led to fraught relations developing between us, but it taught me a valuable lesson which was to prove of considerable use later in life.

Religious instruction took up the whole of the first hour of the school day, and as the afternoons were devoted to clay modelling and occasionally the construction of raffia mats, little food was available to feed the hungry intellect. At another village school where an old friend was educated in those days, the class was being told before Easter the crucifixion story, in great and dramatic detail. The teacher's peroration at last reached its climax: 'Jesus was then laid down upon the cross and nails were struck into his poor hands until he cried out in pain. The blood flowed freely and the cross was raised. More nails were then struck into his feet until he hung in agony, the tears flowing freely from his dear eyes.'

The class listened in rapt attention. Suddenly from the back of the room a village lad who never attended church and for whom the Easter story was new, spoke out into the rapt silence the two words 'the boogers!'

After prayers, the Catechism and religious instruction, there was a little time before the afternoon handwork session to get on with the more serious work of the day. The screens were closed between the two classes and our poor uncertificated supplementary teacher tried to keep us amused. When paper was short, slates were issued, but little was done to any educational advantage.

Poor Mary's arithmetic was weak and she did her best to bridge the gap until noon by teaching a class of mixed ability covering a four-year age span. having no more than the sketchiest of backgrounds herself of the arithmetic and English she was supposed to impart to us. But the afternoon session was to bring her some relief. A large tea chest was hauled out containing grey London clay, which smelt of the sweaty hands of previous generations of scholars. A chunk of this offensive material was deposited on the desk with the imprint of yesterday's efforts still unobliterated, and we set to work. At least this was easier than writing, for the unplaned wooden ridges of the desks were better adapted to slate than pen and pencil.

I sat next to Frankie Weston. Frank and his sister were mentally retarded (there was much dark talk of close interbreeding of village families in those days). When four o'clock came and the church clock across the road chimed, the sound penetrated Frank's misty consciousness and he would say 'It's strook'. It was his only contribution to the whole day's events, so we awaited this declaration with eager anticipation. The clay was rolled up and the two hours of utter boredom was behind us until it was reissued on the next afternoon.

When summer came there was to be a blessed relief from the sticky London clay, for we were introduced to the lighter local variety. The vicar, who was the Chairman of the Managers, had a large walled garden which was badly neglected. He suggested to the Headmaster that it would be to the advantage of all concerned if the boys learned the principles of gardening. As winter came to its end we were marched over to the vicarage and the garden was divided into a number of substantial plots. The boys were paired and each pair allocated a plot. We were taught double digging, a heavy labour even for a grown man and a massive one for lads of our age. Frankie was strong, however, and between us we manfully toiled away on two or three afternoons a week. We were then instructed in the planting of potatoes, peas beans and other vegetables. Most of the boys were already accustomed to the work, as they helped their fathers in the evenings. The crops matured, the vicar and the headmaster benefited substantially, and as we clamped the potatoes for the winter we wondered whether our labours would be recompensed. But there was no such luck.

One or two brighter or more adventurous spirits scrumped some apples, but their only reward was the cane. The school inspector was also paid off with a generous gift of vegetables. There was no national curriculum in those days. But at least we were beginning to learn something of life. Years later I was to reflect upon the apocryphal story of the headmaster who lined up all the new boys in the quadrangle on the first day of term. 'Now, boys' he said, 'Bend over'. Dutifully they did so, and he struck each of them with a firm whack of the cane.

'Boys' he said, 'That is the first, and I might add the most important, lesson that you will ever learn in this school - that life is unfair.'

So Frankie and I laboured away our summer afternoons among the vicar's cabbages. In the mornings, as the brightest boy in the class and the only one to proceed to the grammar school, I was seated next to Frankie to 'help him along'. Behind us sat Nitty Reynolds. Nitty's head was regularly shaven because of a perennial infestation of head lice. His great enemy was the 'dick nurse' and Nitty would hide in the lavatory on her arrival until he felt it safe to emerge.

The poorest family was the Kibbler tribe, who lived in a labourer's cottage beyond the village. When we were presented with a mongrel puppy. Mr Kibbler was sent for and for three pence he removed the tail with his teeth. Spitting out a mouthful of fleas which he had allegedly found, he demanded an extra penny and a cup of tea to 'wash them down'. The dog became my constant companion and on Sunday I would take him out together with Monty Brickwood, who supplemented his meagre pay as village roadsweeper and linksman by ratcatching. One Sunday morning, with help from Monty's ferrets, we caught half a dozen rats. Each time he caught one the tail was removed against the one penny bounty paid by the local council. And each time one went into the sack Monty would say 'There, another fucker.' As far as I was concerned, this was a new and sophisticated figure of speech, so when I arrived home for Sunday lunch and my father asked me how we had got on I said 'we caught six fuckers' assuming that this word was synonymous with rat. I was to my great chagrin, not allowed out again with Monty.

Ratcatching on a larger scale took place at many of the farms when the threshing machine arrived, and armed with sticks we would surround each rick as the old sheaves were removed. Towards the bottom of the rick, the last few layers exuded a musty smell and nests of rats and mice would be uncovered. Dogs and sticks hounded the unfortunate creatures and there was great sport. At these times and at harvest, the school attendance record declined and there, was a spate of colds, influenza and other minor ills. Many years later, as a headmaster myself, I had occasion to send for a parent who produced a medical certificate for her frequently absent son which read 'Influenza, ipse dixit'. Well Mrs Innes' I said 'I'm sorry to hear Freddie has had the flu.'

'Yes 'edmaster' she replied. 'But I don't really know whether he's had the ipsy dixit.'

At the village school it became apparent that I was not progressing as well as I might under the supplementary teacher's instruction, and although mother's influence as the infants' teacher was brought to bear, it was some time before it was agreed that I might fare better in the senior class of children aged eleven to fourteen. So at the tender age of nine I was promoted. I was to find the company socially, if not academically, sophisticated. Sex in particular was not a matter in which I had been tutored at home but more of that later. On one morning an inspector arrived at the school. The headmaster had anticipated his visit and we had learned some scraps of doggerel against such a contingency. One piece was entitled 'My poor dog Tray' and another began 'Oh mother how lovely the moon looks tonight'. I was hauled out before the class and told to recite. I came up with Leigh Hunt's *Abou Ben Adhem*, which I had learned at home and knew word perfect. The inspector congratulated the headmaster on his choice of verse and the day was saved. But after he left the premises the matter was not referred to again and we continued to learn juvenile nursery rhymes. Later at the grammar school those of my generation were to learn a great deal of verse, much of which I can still recite. Geoffrey Stone, who was an inspector of schools in Northern Ireland, tells two stories of the casual approach to education in earlier days. As a matter of some urgency he was asked to visit a small and isolated school in the heart of the Sperrin Mountains. He sent a note to the Headmistress to say that he would arrive on the following Tuesday. The weather on the day was dreadful, with low cloud and steady snowfall. After a difficult journey he arrived to find the school empty and locked. Making his way to the headmistress's house nearby, he rang the bell.

'Did you receive my note?' he asked.

'Sure I did' came the reply. 'But when I saw the weather I said to myself Mr Stone would never be such a fool as to come up here on a day like this.'

Even so, education was moving ahead. A school inspector, a new live wire, came to our village having heard something of the doings in more exalted places and suggested that we might have a house system. Accordingly the pupils were allocated to four houses on a regional basis called the Church, the Hill, the Green, and the Nurseries, which reflected residence in various parts of the village. House points were to be given for various achievements, academic as well as athletic, and a weekly total was to be competitively declared. All went well for a while, but before long gang fights began in the playground. The new system had begun to crystallise into a welcome basis for tribal loyalties and internecine warfare, particularly as the Nursery lads, who now called themselves the 'Nussers', had a recruitment of farmers' sons who resented the Green boys, who largely lived on a newly-built council estate. The social life of the school, once so peaceful, had been provided with a new focus. After a month or two the house system was abandoned as its less savoury implications became apparent to the headmaster.

But my promotion to the senior class was to provide me with other and more stimulating experiences. I had not yet been made aware of what in those days we called euphemistically the 'facts of life'. Sex was then, as a word itself, not usually uttered in polite circles, and when I remarked upon the juxtaposition of two copulating flies in the classroom there was much mysterious laughter. Two fourteen-year-old girls, Doris Sadler and Alice Punte, both well endowed for their years, sat behind me in class. From time to time when the headmaster was out of the room, Alice would unexpectedly shoot her hand up Doris's skirt and into the crutch of her knickers and shout 'I've got her butter, I've got her butter!' (or was it 'button'?) As we had only margarine at home in those stringent times I could not help feeling jealous. I could not appreciate the implications of Alice's lubricious discovery, although these frequent forays, together with the dim and distant recollections of infancy when a nursemaid had guided my tiny fingers, began to awaken half-informed ideas about pleasures not yet understood, still less anticipated.

Nevertheless there were other more immediate high days and holidays to look forward to. At Crow feast, a travelling fair visited the village with its roundabouts and swings. An ancient steam organ provided the music at decibel levels rarely heard in those days, and the school was given a holiday. At the village in a neighbouring county visited by the fair, the occasion of the Silver Jubilee of King George V and Queen Mary coincided with the 'local feast. It was decided that a tree should be planted on the village green to mark the great day. The honour of the planting was given, after great deliberation, to the oldest inhabitant. Old George had never before attended a public function, and here he was surrounded by all the local hierarchy and squirearchy. George was asked to say a few words.

Never before had he been faced with such a demand. His face and neck reddened beneath his weatherbeaten labourer's tan as he summoned up his courage.

'Well' he averred 'I've planted this 'ere tree and I 'opes the bugger grows.'

George, as sexton, was not unaccustomed to the use of the spade and he liked his pint of beer. One warm summer evening, digging a late grave for a funeral on the morrow, he slipped across the road for a drink to slake his thirst. In convivial company one pint led to another, and it was dark when he staggered across the churchyard to collect his spade.

After he had collected his equipment, he sat down in the open grave for a rest and fell asleep. Early the following misty morning in the half light, two labourers were taking a short cut across the churchyard on the way to work when George awoke. Peering out of the open grave he called out 'Can you tell us the time mate?'

The generation brought up in country villages in the years between the wars was far closer to the Victorians in its mores and social life than those of today. Those who remain catch echoes and memories of the past which have long since disappeared. We would have felt equally at home in Victorian or Edwardian times. There was little traffic on the roads. Ponies and traps clattered along the lanes. Horses worked the fields and most families were employed on the land. An aeroplane flying over was an event and a journey beyond the local town an occasion to be long anticipated and remembered.

Oil lamps lit our homes, and when the gas main arrived in later years we had one gas light installed in the living room. Water, for all, was from the pump. As a fortunate family we had our own, but most people drew their supply by bucket from one of the village wells. There was, of course no electricity and all the advantages that stem from that indispensable source of power today. Many families took the weekly joint, if they could afford one, to the bakehouse and on Sunday after church a procession would collect at the end of Water Lane for the weekend joint and Yorkshire pudding.

Heavenly smells wafted out from the baker's on that day. We sniffed them like the Bisto Kids and there would be much gossip and sometimes critical inspection of what other families could or could not afford for Sunday dinner. As we lived a mile or more from the village, we could not make use of the facilities of the bakehouse and cooking had to be done on an oven heated by an open fire. Mother was neither a good nor an enthusiastic cook, and this led to some interesting Sunday mornings which depended on the unpredictable open fire range heated by logs and the lack of her cooking abilities. During the week, because of her teaching duties, she did not cook, and when we returned home after a sandwich lunch we ate fish paste, potted meat, cheese, bread and jam and at weekends, 'shop cake'. These were the convenience foods of those days. On Sunday my sister would dance round the table, as we were to have meat for dinner, while on Saturday father would come home from the town with winkles, pickled herrings, pigs' trotters or some equally inexpensive delicacy for the weekend.

Everything father touched went wrong. Unemployed through the thirties, he tried his hand at a series of disastrous enterprises. A few pounds were saved from mother's meagre salary and a bullnosed Morris of ancient vintage was purchased. A box of sliding trays was constructed by a local carpenter and father made the journey to town daily to purchase cakes from W Q Adams, a local wholesaler, to hawk around the villages. Mother lent him the school handbell on Saturdays and we would sally forth. I would walk ahead ringing the bell as we sold crumpets at the weekend. I felt very important as I walked around the streets calling our wares. We had to be back in the town by the middle of the afternoon, for the cakes were on 'sale or return' and our residue was then sold at W Q Adams' Saturday afternoon tea rooms.

Once or twice the bullnosed Morris broke down and we lived on stale cakes for the rest of the week. This we enjoyed, although it was a minor financial tragedy for Father as his floating capital was all invested in the week's cakes. The unreliability of the car and the uncertainty of the local demand for cakes soon defeated him and brought the enterprise to a close. In those days there was no such thing as social security and the dole was miniscule. Friends whose parents were similarly placed, having been sacked, received no redundancy. The shades of the workhouse still loomed in the background.

Dad did what a later generation might later call a 'Tebbit': he got on his bike and branched out into his old trade of men's outfitting. Nearby Corby was a newly-developed town, mainly populated with steelworkers from Scotland and the North of England skilled in heavy industry and now exploiting the iron ore of the Northamptonshire sandstone. Unfortunately for us they, in turn, exploited Dad. With high hopes he sallied forth, put his bike on the train and, pattern book in hand, took many orders for cheap bespoke suits which he then had made up in the town. But he had not made allowances for the wily Scotsmen, and when the time came for delivery and payment he was often left with an unsaleable suit, made to measure, for which his customer offered a figure far below that originally agreed.

Next he tried hawking orders for beer on a commission basis for Messrs Phipps brewery, which was turning in good profits even in those hard times. Indeed one of the founding fathers of the firm applied some of his gains to the construction of St. Matthew's Church, which was later to be known as Phipps's fire escape. Dad worked his round in tandem with a delivery man, but unhappily his companion had a great thirst for the firm's products and the enterprise collapsed.

One day a stray cockerel wandered into our backyard. It was corralled, and next market day Father made his way to the local cattle market, where he purchased a dozen pullets. We waited with bated breath for the harvest of eggs and probably of chickens that would soon arrive and be our economic salvation, but the cock turned out to be infertile and the eggs never came. Father was not aware of the need to provide the birds with proper living accommodation, so whilst they came to the doorstep for grain they deposited their ovine bounty far and wide in the surrounding hedgerows. From time to time I found nests of addled eggs, so the hens were sold off to the local butcher. No one collected the night soil from the outdoor earth closet at our isolated home and every fortnight Father and I would seek plots further and further afield where we would dig a deep hole by the hedgerow to bury the bucket of shit. Dad lit a Woodbine to create a sanitised smokescreen, as Mother regarded the purchase of disinfectant as wasteful and the unpleasant cargo of turds and newspaper disappeared below ground. The hole was covered and carefully marked as we had had unfortunate relocation problems in the past.

It was on these excursions that we were to discover the secretive habits of our recalcitrant poultry. Needless to say my father never expanded his chicken farm and returned to his scanning of the *Chronicle & Echo* for other possible business opportunities. But life had other outlets and interests, although somewhat simpler than those of today. Not many people had radios, for there was no electricity in the village, and for those who had the good fortune to possess a battery set, accumulators had to be brought from town after being recharged weekly. They were hazardous burdens with their open vents of acid swinging from the back of a bicycle with me on the back seat and Dad up front. When his carbide lamp failed for lack of the water which released the gas from the lumps of carbide, it was my responsibility to pee in the container, which he unscrewed, replaced and relit the lamp. To ride a bike after dark without a lamp in those innocent days was a serious offence and names of offenders and fines levied were regularly reported in the *Chronicle & Echo*. This was the only news most people saw, and national and international events impinged little upon our daily lives.

One day, however, a short distance from our house, a car caught fire. A commercial traveller by the name of Rowse, who had numerous lady friends in different parts of the country, had found their rival claims upon his energies and finances more than he could continue to bear. Seeing a convenient tramp by the roadside, he befriended him, and when the man's back was turned he struck him with the starting handle of the car, thrust him into the driving seat, and leaving his own pocket watch in the waistcoat pocket of his victim, he set the car ablaze with a can of petrol, hoping that the charred remains would be mistaken for his own, enabling him to write off his numerous embarrassing alliances. Unfortunately he was spotted by two late homecomers, and the affair became a celebrated murder case. At the village school I was able to bathe in the reflected glory of our near proximity to the crime. Rowse was hanged.

Our main excursion beyond the village, apart from the necessary shopping expeditions to Northampton, was to Kislingbury, a nearby village where Auntie Fanny lived in sin with her half brother uncle Charlie. Their home was a tiny cottage and uncle was on the dole. He had been an engine cleaner in his younger days at Stockton on Tees and would regale us with stories of life in those times. A staunch Socialist, he would tell us how he was issued with engine rags for cleaning purposes each week with tightly-tied knots in the corners which would be snipped off at the end of the week in order to determine that it was the original piece of railway property and had not been substituted for a cheaper piece of material.

One day, just before we disposed of the bull-nosed Morris, Father won twenty pounds or so on the football pools. It was decided that we would go to the seaside for a week that summer. The nearest place was Frinton, and we proceeded in that direction through Bedford and East Anglia. The car was in bad shape, emitting smoke and noise, and just beyond Bedford we stopped to enquire the way. When we announced our destination, the woman we spoke to looked hard at the vehicle and said 'Well God help you'. This did not inspire confidence, but in spite of this we arrived.

After a diligent search we found lodgings in a nearby village and garaged the car in the garden. Each day we walked to the sea at Frinton to save petrol. In those days it was a most selective resort. Not only did Mother mistrust the car, which was a fitful starter, but there was the additional problem that we should be seen to arrive at the Greensward, as the front was called, among the finer conveyances parked there. This had something to do with an organisation called the CSSM or Children's Special Service Mission, which provided evangelical and more secular diversions for nice children. This was amply confirmed for Mother when she discovered that we would be attached to a group led by young Lord Kenworthy, late of Oundle and Cambridge. I had never met a lord before and was suitably impressed.

Morning services were conducted on the beach daily, tide permitting, from a sandcastle pulpit, and we were encouraged to declare that we had been saved.

At first I was unsure. As a reward for this we were allowed to attend such delights later in the day as sausage suppers, treasure hunts, races and singsongs. Along with several others I thought it wise to declare that I was saved, unless the delights of the afternoon and evening were denied. One day I made friends with a lad on the beach and introduced him to the CSSM authorities, but their hierarchy later discovered that he had not passed his eleven plus and was attending a central school. He was discreetly asked to leave the organisation, with a copy of the New Testament to soften the blow.

As he watched our collective junketings from afar, I pondered in my youthful way upon the politics of salvation as interpreted by our evangelical friends. Two of the leaders did, however correspond with me for some years afterwards, enquiring anxiously about my bible reading habits and the continued state of my salvation. Their motives were most excellent. Following

the summer holiday, I was now to be able to confirm the validity of my membership of the CSSM. I was to enter the new world of the grammar school.

CHAPTER TEN

GRAMMAR SCHOOL DAYS

As I mentioned earlier, George Bernard Shaw once complained that his education had been interrupted by his schooling. For those of us who were at school between the wars who came from humble backgrounds, nothing could be further from the truth when we made the two traumatic transitions, first to grammar schools and later to universities. The impact of Northampton Grammar School, which in those days before its sad decline was represented on the headmasters' conference and ranked as a public school, had a shattering effect on those few lads from remote villages who were fortunate enough to gain a place.

An even finer filter awaited those few of us who managed later to go to the older universities. The very size of the building was greater than any we had entered before. Like mediaeval pilgrims entering a cathedral, we shrank in size. The masters in their tattered gowns, the rigours of the academic discipline, the expectations of homework, the huge men who were to be our prefects, the oval footballs, the Eton collars and clerical grey suits, the straw boaters in summer, the parades of the cadet corps, all conspired to overawe the little newcomers from their remote country places. Situated high above the valley of the River Nene with its spacious playing fields on the river terraces, it was by far the most prestigious boys' school for miles around. Two forms of scholarship boys and one of fee payers provided the only avenue for the able or fortunate boy to proceed to higher education in those days in a town of over a hundred thousand and its neighbouring county region. We were indeed a privileged minority. With the legacy of the village school behind me, I managed to achieve a place one from the bottom of the top form in the first year. But by the end of the second year I had won the form prize for first place in the same form.

Like so many of that generation, we owed a great deal to fine and dedicated teachers. Brasso of the cadet force, who taught French, Cabbage Lily, Skinny, Ben, Gussy, Toss, Nack, Foe, Hell – everyone had a nickname. At the helm was 'Pimp' Cooke. Pimp recruited each year a cherubic first former to attend his study after morning prayers as fag to run early errands. They were known as Pimp's bum boys, but I don't think this was anything more than a schoolboys' sobriquet. The nearest he ever got to our bottoms was the feared administration of the 'whack', which was liberally applied in those days. But more than in most professions, teachers must catch the accents of tomorrow if they are to open out the sympathies and imaginations of the young, and many of the staff in those pre-war grammar schools did just that.

Many of us were 'accelerated' and took the school certificate and matriculation examination, the equivalent of the present GCSE, in four years, the majority then leaving school. Most of these today would have proceeded to universities, and at the age of 14 or 15 went into 'safe' jobs in local banks or insurance offices. This then was the tiny few who had gained places at the local grammar school, and only a very few of these had parents who were prepared to look towards a career to university and beyond.

The under-education of potential talent was appalling and a loss to both individual and nation. The Somme had taken some of the best, under-education failed the survivors and their progeny, and much of the responsibility for the running of the country's great enterprises and its politics fell perforce into the often less talented hands which had been fed by money and privilege. Little wonder that we were so miserably badly governed by the many incompetents who sat in the seats of power in the 1930s.

And indeed more sinister things were happening in the world during those years beyond the walls of our schools. As we became aware of this, sides were taken in such things as the Spanish Civil War and as the Italian invasion of Abyssinia progressed we sang:

> *The Duce gives the order*
> *And the organ grinders go*
> *To the front in Abyssinia*
> *To fight the native foe*
> *But alas the organ grinders*
> *Will never grind again*
> *For they've left their grinding organs*
> *On the Abyssinian plains.*

A number of our contemporaries joined the Air Cadets. Many of these were to die later in the Battle of Britain as pilots.

A school visit to Germany in 1936 for some of us who were taking a second foreign language opened eyes to the reality of the gathering storm. But in those days we were more concerned with the local bullies than the international variety. One particular bully decided to try me out. His nickname, for reasons which will become apparent, was Tug. His expertise was an unpleasant and often painful exercise known in the schoolboy vernacular of those days as pilling. Unexpectedly he would suddenly appear from behind his victim and grab him by his recently descended testicles. Having suffered on more than one occasion, I resolved that next time I would give fight. The master on duty, who had presumably observed this unattractive habit of common assault, ignored the fight as I set upon him. That and my inclusion in the year's rugby side ensured that the bullies steered clear of me.

The dawning of sexual reality in those days was not subject to the sort of stimulus that boys are exposed to today. It was largely confined to rather crude jokes amongst us, while contact with the opposite sex was very restricted. There was some gentle proselytising from form masters. On one occasion when a boy was playing with his member on the back row the master said 'I should save that, my boy, until you grow up'.

'I do so, sir' he whispered, sotto voce so most of us heard him, 'I keep it in a jam jar at home.'

But sex, as such, did not rear what was then described as its ugly head until most of us reached the sixth form. By that time it was beginning to dawn upon us that deeper and darker waters lay around us. Jack Hubbard and I - Jack was later to follow me with the same exhibition at Jesus College Oxford - were both cherubic and younger than our sixth form years. Invited to a local go club by a member of the town council, we went innocently to his home to drink cider and listen to the latest jazz records. We were then invited up to his bedroom to experiment with chest developers. It soon became apparent that his motives were impure, and Jack and I, both confirmed heterosexuals, left in haste. The councillor later moved away to run a boys' club in Birmingham. My next encounter was with a local vicar, later to become a prince of the church, who invited me to visit him on numerous occasions and eventually, to my astonishment, threw me to the floor in his drawing room. By this time I was in the fifteen at school and managed to escape and fight off his advances.

When I had been much younger and had first entered the grammar school, I had had another encounter with the proprietor of a local cycle repair shop. When I proffered my shilling for the repair of a puncture, he took me into his workshop and without further ado unbuttoned his flies to display the largest erect member I have ever seen. As my astonished eyes gazed at this vast organ, the like of which I had never beheld erect before, he said 'Its a bloody good 'un'. I began to understand that the world was a more complicated place than I had thought.

I was now becoming more interested in what the other sex had to offer. Certainly we were far less sexually sophisticated in those days, back in the thirties. When the war came and many of the men left for the services, some of the older girls took an interest in those of us who were still in the sixth form at school.

There were occasions when hands were directed by willing feminine fingers toward the more delectable parts of the female anatomy, but ignorance and fear of the consequences deterred us from taking advantage of such inviting offers. There were undoubtedly those who would have echoed the Catholic maiden's prayer:

Mary mother I believe
Without sin thou didst conceive
Mother Mary still believing
Let me sin without conceiving.

Alternatively there was never any opportunity to emulate the apocryphal Uncle George and Auntie Mabel:

…Who fainted at the breakfast table
And took that as a solemn warning
Not to do it in the morning
Ovaltine has put them right
And now they do it morn and night
And Uncle George has promised soon
To do it in the afternoon.

Necking, as it was called, fell short of the more intimate delights enjoyed by a more liberated post-war generation, so we discovered and put up with the discomforts of sustained and unsatisfied erections, either on the dance floor or after the long walk home. Footsteps that echo along the corridors of memory towards doors which were ajar but never opened.

Even at a day school in those times, we were well segregated for most of the week from the opposite sex, and the sixth forms were small in number. Only a handful stayed on with the intention in most cases of passing professional examinations into such careers as the Civil Service, some to teachers' training colleges and a few to the provincial universities. There were no grants available unless you signed the pledge that you intended to teach. This was an undertaking with the Board of Education that in exchange you were prepared to enter the teaching profession. The only hope of a free ride to a possible glittering prize was either one of the few State Scholarships or better an open award at Oxford or Cambridge. Many such awards were restricted to the ancient public schools, which picked up most of the open awards as well. Oxbridge filled up its places with fee-paying commoners, many of whom had a bare matriculation qualification.

But from time to time one of us would win an open award and then try to supplement the scholarship income with anything that might be added by the generosity of the county or a school trust. Our hopes were high, but there was no royal road to success as there is today, when a clutch of good A levels is the first step to a place in the sun.

But overshadowing all else was the declaration of war in 1939. Some of the best and most able younger members of the staffs of the schools left for the forces and were replaced by the wives of staff and others who came back from retirement.

A further complication for the more safely located provincial schools was the advent of the evacuees. Kilburn Grammar School and Willesden Grammar School arrived in Northampton and our formal education became restricted to mornings only. This was not a very auspicious start to sixth form work. We began to see more of our guests from North London as the early days of the 'phony war' progressed. They seemed to be more sophisticated and streetwise than we country cousins. A place for evening work called Youth House was opened for them and a club to be called the Roadmender as a social centre. We soon integrated with them and they provided a new dimension of city education which did us no harm. Richard Baker, the television newsreader, who later served on the staff of the school of which I was to become headmaster, was a leading light from Kilburn and there were many others who brought a new stimulus from London, especially the girls.

Evacuees also arrived in the village, and I was asked to help in settling them by mother, who was then teaching at the village school. The arrival of the pathetic small souls from London primary schools with gas masks around their necks, clutching their tiny talismans, teddy bears and dolls was heartrending. With their tearstained faces we were soon to gather that many of them had never been away from home before. Then began a process of social selection, with the cleaner and apparently more docile children finding their way to the better off families. Some of the village homes were rough and ready. Some were hard and even harsh. Beds were wetted, children were beaten, food was not always adequate. But in some cases lifelong associations were formed between foster parents and their charges. We had done our best, but within a year or so a large number of our charges had returned to London and the bombs.

As the war continued and continental Europe fell to Hitler, things began to deteriorate. Food rationing became more severe and friends left for the services, while those of us who had entered the sixth form at fifteen and were not yet of military call-up age helped on the local farms during the holidays.

A stray German aircraft fired a few bursts as we stooked wheat at Quinton and bombs fell in the village as enemy planes jettisoned their unspent cargo from raids on Coventry and other Midland towns. School rugby and cricket fixtures were curtailed through lack of petrol and we travelled to our 1st 15 matches in a bus powered by coal gas. In spite of all this we enjoyed our days at school, although the prospect of what was soon to come for most of us as the war developed cast a dark shadow and gave relevance to the old Chinese curse 'May you live in interesting times'. What follows is just by way of illustration, and for contrast with today of the problems faced by those who lacked resources before the universities opened their gates to all who had a minimal qualification.

Expecting to proceed to London University, I entered for the university Inter BSc in Economics. I was 17. Having passed, it soon became clear that money was to be a major obstacle. But a way out was brought to my notice. Open awards were available at Oxford, but only in one of my subsidiary subjects, geography. I entered, with little hope, and went up to Jesus college to take the papers on a succession of cold winter days.

The first paper was an English essay entitled 'The European Tradition' and we were given three hours. I missed the classical allusion and concentrated on the colonial diaspora of settlement and the curse of nationalism. There were other papers in two languages and. our chosen subjects.

To my astonishment a letter arrived a few days later offering me an open exhibition. But money remained a problem. Indeed, my late and dear friend Antony Franklin, who accompanied me up to the line in the 8th Army and was killed, had to turn down an award at Cambridge and then accepted one at Oxford at a less expensive college. Fortunately for me the school governors, having given the school a half holiday to celebrate, decided to give me an exhibition of £25 a year and the county weighed in with A Major County Scholarship of £40. It was still not enough to meet the cost of Oxford in those days. I consequently wrote to the Board of Education and somewhat unwillingly signed the pledge to become a teacher. This produced a state grant and the £205 cobbled up enough to make Oxford a reality. There were other difficulties; I had two foreign languages but no Latin. The college averred that I must gain a pass in Latin, so I set to work and in six months had a grade A in the matriculation examination.

One final hurdle faced all of us in those days. This was the pressing matter of the war. By volunteering to join a regiment in advance of the call up, we were given an undertaking that if we passed the services' Certificate B examination in the University OTC we would be sent straight to an Officer Cadet Training Unit. This seemed a good idea, so I went to the recruiting office and volunteered to join the Queen's Royal Regiment and took the shilling. Now I was at last free to go up to the university, at least until I reached the age when I was due to join the services. Such were the problems that so many of that generation had to overcome to pass through the needle's eye into the halls of future prospects. They are indeed fortunate today when three good A levels sets them on the royal road.

The last term at school passed uneventfully. Money was still in short supply. With two friends at school we held a conference. Ralph Hudson was later to be best man at my wedding. He was to join me at Oxford and then to leave for Chalk River in Canada, where as a physicist he was involved in the production of the atom bomb. He later did distinguished work at the National Physical Laboratory in Washington. Trevor Philpott, after Cambridge, went to the BBC as a commentator with his own programme *The Philpott File* on TV.

We set ourselves up as a consortium to run dances for the local youth. We hired the masonic hall and we called ourselves

'Dances that are different incorporated'. At half a crown a ticket with a hundred or two takers a time, we became rich beyond our then very limited dreams.

Ralph had other talents. He was later to be one of the instigators of the famous Merton hoax, when a number of scholarship candidates at the end of the Michaelmas term, on arrival at the college, were summoned for interview by a panel of postgraduates impersonating the dons. Warned of the interview on the evening of arrival and pre empting the examination, they were grilled with increasingly outrageous questions about their personal lives. Such were our innocent diversions.

For me the time had come to leave the village and enter a more sophisticated milieu, where as an innocent abroad I would certainly have been taken in by a hoax of that sort.

CHAPTER ELEVEN

OXFORD, MORIBUND

The flavour of life in wartime at the University, said my travelling companion as we changed trains at Bletchley, is moribund. In spite of my Exhibition I was not quite sure what he meant and I resolved to look the word up when I arrived at college. He was in some measure right. Many of us were still below age for military service, from which most undergraduates reading pure sciences were exempted as they had other contributions to make to the war effort. They were, in the main, directed into some of the essential secret work that was proceeding in radar, atomic research and such fields. So the colleges were reasonably full. However, few of those reading other subjects stayed on for more than a year with the promise of a place held open for them at the end of the war if they survived. As in the First World War, many of them did not. With few exceptions they were commissioned in one of the three services, and in the great majority of instances at the sharp end of war.

A substantial number of us went to Guards regiments, and when later during my own service in the 8th Army I saw the casualty lists after the Salerno landings they read like an excerpt from Debrett. My own fortunate survival as an infantry subaltern was marred by the deaths of my two closest friends, Alan Docherty and Antony Franklin. So were cut off not only potentially brilliant individual careers, but once again a disproportionate loss of the talent and energy which the nation would sorely need in peacetime was to be missing.

At Oxford the quadrangles had lost their lawns, their places now filled with static water tanks. One night in 1941 when the German Air Force was engaged in what were known as the Baedeker raids, we were told that Oxford was the intended target. But the weather closed in and we were stood down from an expected night's fire fighting. The leaking of this information of the enemy's intentions had filtered through to the University from Enigma information gathered at Bletchley. A similar 'leak' was passed from King George the 6th to Eton college on another occasion, but there was always a reluctance for these scraps of potentially life-saving intelligence from the Enigma analysts at Bletchley to be passed down the line in case the Germans were to gain knowledge of the insecurity of their cypher systems. Harry Golombek, the chess master and one of my old boys, told me many years later that when he was at Bletchley Park this was to be a bone of serious contention and concern between Churchill and the services.

Quite rightly, there was tight security preventing the leakage of scraps of intelligence, even if it might save lives, if it risked raising enemy suspicions that we had the ultimate key to their codes. Fortunately we had no need to use the static water tanks, although on one high-spirited evening after a practice hose drill, when it was judged that our old rivals across the Turl might be going into hall for dinner, a high-power jet crossed the street from the front quadrangle into Exeter. They were not amused, and nor was Percy Seymore, our Junior Dean, and he let us know it.

In spite of all the necessary diminutions of style and substance that wartime conditions inflicted upon the University, the effect of the place on boys like myself coming from a home with no electricity, bedrooms lit by candlelight, water from an outdoor pump and an outdoor lavatory was considerable. With but one living room and two small bedrooms and my father unemployed since the slump, I found the sudden transition, even to wartime Oxford with dinner in hall surrounded by college silver, a personal servant (my scout), access to a bathroom, the blessings of electricity and the privacy of my own suite of rooms almost overwhelming. Here were people who regularly travelled beyond the nearest town, while some had even ventured abroad. Here were debates in the Union where luminaries such as Hore Belisha, then Secretary of State for War and Wellington Koo, the Chinese Ambassador were to speak, and from the floor we could try to catch the Speaker's eye. Here later, as Secretary of the University Geographical Society (the Herbertson Society), I was to entertain to dinner Peter Fleming the writer, and dine Anton Walbrook, the actor, in hall at Jesus. Walbrook's interest in one of my friends after this occasion confirmed our view that he was best avoided. Nevertheless all this was heady stuff at the time and a quantum leap from the village I had so recently left.

We all, like so many generations before, began to make lifelong friendships with some who were to reach eminence in their own fields. I would share tutorials with a man who was to become a King (Seretse Khama of Bechuanaland) and later share tables with three of our future Prime Ministers.

Perhaps the one thing we lacked when we were compared with our contemporaries from some of the more distinguished public schools was confidence in ourselves, but we had at least given the door a good hard kick.

The pattern of the day and week was somewhat of a surprise. My large and commodious sitting and dining room were shared with a Blundellian called John Coyte, late of a minor public boarding school, who informed me that boys at that school were prepared to sell themselves for a postage stamp. Although he put no specific poundage on this, I found the information rather alarming, as we were destined to live in close proximity, especially as I was not so inclined. But I was soon relieved to discover that John was an enthusiastic heterosexual.

We were woken by our scout, Bill Hammond, with an early morning cup of tea and listened to him as he prepared to lay the fire and light it in our room on staircase VII, which had been occupied at one time, as he told us, by a well-known bishop. As I got to know John I thought it unlikely that the present occupants would emulate their predecessor. In any case the odour of sanctity soon dispersed in the currency of our tenure.

Later in the year, when Bill's 'emerods' smote him, Alf West became responsible for our creature comforts. One of Alf's young men had become Lawrence of Arabia, and by now it was entirely clear to me that John's proclivities related more closely to the literary expositions of the other Lawrence and were not even, as I had feared, ambisextrous.

In those days the introduction of women into college was a matter fraught with potential disaster. A contemporary who had a deep and sincere interest in the anatomy of the opposite sex shared his room with a devout undergraduate with the name of King. The latter came in unexpectedly in the afternoon to find Eric busily involved on the carpet with a very nubile undergraduette. Meeting in the Junior Common room that evening, King challenged Eric and said 'I was shocked to find you behaving in our room in that manner this afternoon, I don't know what could have come over you. What do you think you would have said if you had found me behaving like that?' With no hesitation Eric replied 'Oh, 'I'd have just said 'Good King, whence this lass?'

But to return to the day. After a leisurely breakfast we would attend lectures, rarely more than three or four a week. Some we sampled for the first week or so of term, only to abandon the less well delivered. The academic high point of the week, then as today, was the tutorial. I saw J N L Baker in his rooms for this exercise, but more interesting was tea on a Sunday afternoon at his home in Headington, where he lived with his two beautiful daughters, one later to become Baroness Young and leader of the House of Lords.

Most afternoons were spent on the field or the river, and for other diversions we joined the usual diverse clubs and societies. One of the few organisations that ran a monthly hop was the Democratic Socialists. This seemed to be a good enough reason for joining, although my friends and I did not attend the political sessions. As I had learned to play the piano at school, I was in demand as a jazz pianist at their monthly frolics. After an afternoon at play we ate our cream cakes from the buttery, dined on hall, and like all the generations before us talked late into the night. Occasions such as a success on field or river or a 21st birthday merited celebration, and on St David's Day, which brought out the worst in the Welsh contingent at Jesus, Englishmen would be evicted bodily through the windows of the Junior Common Room.

On these festive evenings there was heavy 'sconcing' on hall. This was adjudicated by the senior Exhibitioner on our table and offences which merited this sanction were mostly bad manners at table. From what I have seen in more recent years when dining in numerous academic institutions, it would be good sense if such cautionary customs still prevailed. The mention of any woman's name other than that of the founder, Elizabeth, also attracted a fine of a two-pint sconce in one of the ancient and priceless silver college tankards. The miscreant could, however, appeal in Latin to High Table. Few succeeded. If permission was granted by the senior man at table, the offender could attempt to drain the sconce. This involved drinking it in one draught and was not easy to achieve. I had not tasted beer until I went up and to drink a quart of College Old straight down was something of an achievement, and a folly. But it was done from time to time. The senior man then had to buy a sconce himself.

Sconces were more usually passed round the table, and much conviviality resulted until the presentation of the 'battels' bill at end of term. The authorities would look with some disfavour upon an over-large bar bill. My old friend Phimister, later in life a most respected headmaster of Mill Hill, whispered to me as we put him to bed, 'Norman, I'm only twenty one but I wish I were dead'. Fortunately he survived to follow a distinguished career.

At Jesus there was, and still is, a society known as the Elizabethan, or Lizzie for short. Entry to this was restricted to some of the heavier drinking sportsmen of the college. Their activities were uncivilised at times, as for example when a quantity of beer somehow found its way into the works of the college clock. After piously singing hymns, we would repair to the JCR on a Sunday evening for a sing-song, when such classics as *Angeline* (sweet sixteen), *Cathusalem* (the harlot of Jerusalem), *Mr Banglestein* (balls to) the old Rajah of Astakhan (a bit of a bugger, a hell of a man), *Ringarangaroo* (oh what is that, it's big and black like a pussy cat) the man with no balls at all and other such ditties followed the mellifluous Welsh rendering of hymns in chapel.

I was co-opted as 'court tinkler' for the society and in consequence had the verses, many of them pages long, imprinted indelibly on my mind. I do not think it did me any moral harm and it was to stand me in good stead when I later became an army officer.

For the war was soon to cast a lengthening. shadow over our sunlit afternoons on the river and playing fields. The price we were to pay for our short respite was soon to be exacted. For a day and a half each week we were soldiers in the OTC. Certificates A and B were required for our passage to Officer Cadet Training Units. Others were recruited into the University Air Squadron or the 'Y' scheme, which was the channel for naval commissions. We were indeed the last of the blue-eyed boys who were to go down from the universities after a year and have no other rank service.

On an August day in 1942, wearing university blazers, we arrived at our OCTUs. Another and much sterner chapter had opened. Yet all of this has been recounted in earlier chapters. We had had our first days as freshmen, to be followed by years of soldiering. The time was later to come for us to meet the challenge of the reconstruction of a bankrupt country trying to find a role in a new world where the territory ahead was even more uncharted than that which my father had faced at the end of the first internecine conflict in Europe.

CHAPTER TWELVE

GELDED YOUTH

And so, as described earlier in this saga, the golden lads and lasses who had survived the conflict and returned to the universities faced the future with the country's economy in shreds and the socialists in the saddle riding a badly wounded horse. My tutor at Jesus tried to point me towards a trainee managers' course at Marks and Spencer, Commonwealth Fund Fellowships or a research post graduateship for a further degree at Oxford.

Once again it was all a matter of finding the necessary finance. I wrote to the then Ministry of Education asking if, with my tutor's support, I might read a B. Litt or submit a thesis for a D. Phil degree. I had opted to teach when I had accepted a grant to boost my income from scholarships, and as far as they were concerned I had better honour this and read a Diploma in Education. In the vernacular of the times, this agreement was known as the pledge.

The course proved to be a year spent in enjoyable and relaxed surroundings. I had fallen in love with the beautiful daughter of the deputy Chief Constable of Northampton, Bill Afford, and we had married. She and I, together with my best man, Ralph Hudson of Merton, were back at Oxford. Ralph had helped to produce the atom bomb as one of the Chalk

River team in Canada. Together with him and his Canadian wife, we rented a cottage just outside Oxford. Ralph worked at the Clarendon Laboratories for his Doctorate and I read my Plato. A good time was had by all. But only too soon the day dreaded by so many alumni loomed, when the need to earn a living approached. Later, more fortunate generations were able to delay the academipause, but in our time there was a pressing need for a contribution to be made to the commonweal. The war was over, the cupboard was bare and in the country's parlous state, the need for people to take off their jackets and get down to work was desperate. In the later days of more open-handed grants to graduates there were those among my headmaster colleagues who wondered whether the pendulum of prodigality had swung too far in the other direction sometimes, in not a few cases subsidising the mediocre from the public purse.

An *éminence grise* in the world of education in these post-war years was A R Woolley, then the Secretary of the Oxford University Appointments Board. I was not the only one to fall into the *grise* of his eminence, but this was my own fault. Notices of vacancies at public schools were sorted through his filters. As a brash young man returning from the war I had sought an interview at his offices during my discharge leave from the army. In service dress and Sam Browne and with captain's pips on my shoulders I attended his headquarters at the appointed time.

It may be recalled that I had already at the age of 22 been responsible for the army welfare services in three Italian cities, running a large budget and with perhaps too much responsibility and power for my immaturity to carry. I was not accustomed to be kept waiting, but in fairness to myself I was not accustomed to keep others waiting either. After half an hour or more had elapsed, I asked Woolley's secretary to take a message to him and remind him of my presence. We did not hit it off. Two years later, his filters were applied. Two posts fell vacant, one at Bedford school and one at Bedford Modern, both public schools, but the latter at the time less prestigious and less well paid. I received no notification of the former, which went to an Oxford contemporary lower in the class list but a nice man from a better stable. I applied for the job at Bedford Modern and was appointed. I never regretted it and spent ten of the happiest years of my life there.

A few years later I was to apply for a sixth form mastership at Merchant Tailors School. I was offered the post by the then Headmaster, Hugh Elder. Reluctantly I had to turn the job down. London house prices were then beyond our means. Woolley's private reference was sent back to me in error. It was not a bad one, but the sting was in the tail which read 'Unfortunately he speaks with a slight Midland accent'.

To Elder's credit, this apparently didn't matter. As in my village schooldays when I had had the temerity to correct the Headmaster as a young Galileo, I had learnt another important lesson in life. It is not what you know and always even who you know, but how you approach those who know they know better.

The first I was to get to know among these was the Headmaster of Bedford Modern School, Mr J E Taylor. Bedford in the immediate post-war years was a small market town of great charm. Latterly, in common with similar places of like nature, it has been allowed to grow beyond that optimum size with which mankind seems better able to relate. The Harpur Trust administers the four public schools and the two boys' academies live today in friendly rivalry. But back in the first half of the century when Grose-Hodge came to Bedford school as Headmaster, he was told that the academic establishment of the town was redolent with snobbery. He was quoted as saying 'I will show them what snobbery really is'! At Bedford Modern, which had kept its old name of Modern in spite of the emergence of the then new secondary modern schools, we were inclined to believe that there was some truth in this.

Despite the presence of Dickie Jeeps, later to captain England, in the first XV, it was unthinkable that the two schools should meet on the rugby field at that level. We felt rather like those who faced:

The regiment from Poona
That would infinitely sooner
Play single-handed polo
A sort of solo polo
Than play a single chukka
With a chap who isn't pukka.

The playing fields lay beyond the town where the new school now stands. They were reached by bicycle, which for nearly all was the sole form of locomotion in the town. Only the rich, like the wealthy housemasters, possessed cars.

The old school, now long since demolished except for its external facade, was in the centre of Bedford. From the surrounding streets it looked very much like an Oxford or Cambridge college. Inside, the main quadrangle and cloisters had the air of a prison yard in which the inmates were kept in seclusion from the town and its temptations behind great oaken doors. Parents were excluded from the campus, their only access being through a small side door leading to the Headmaster's study. As a junior member of the staff I began to wonder whether any of the boys had parents. In ten years at the school I was never to meet any on the premises to discuss with them their boys' progress, or lack of it. This was not uncommon in the public schools of that day. They were kept at arm's length from the assistant staff and only met the Head or the Housemasters.

J E Taylor, JET as he was known, was not the very model of a modern headmaster but rather that of a very Victorian one. He was a great admirer of Arnold of Rugby, and sometimes I wondered if he had admired the formidable Dr Keate, who flogged Eton into submission. He ran the school along the lines of a benevolent dictatorship. But he had standards, and they were more authoritarian times than those of today. My own view later in a similar office was much in accord with his - that if you were to administer an oligarchy it was all right as long as you were Olly. He had been the third in a succession of three generations of headmasters of Sir Walter St John's Grammar school in London and had been known as the Father Son and Holy Spirit. Taylor had plenty of spirit and could, when roused, inspire holy terror. The cane was wielded vigorously by all and sundry, including the monitors. He would cheerfully have whacked the staff if that had been allowed, and deservedly lashed some of us with his tongue.

Lock up at night for boarders and day boys was strictly enforced after 6 pm, with a brief extension to 8 pm in high summer. If you broke this rule, the reward was inevitably the stick. Parents hid their sons beneath blankets on the back seats of cars when returning from late evening safaris. Monitors patrolled the evening streets like the bulldogs of Oxford. The girls from the two girls' public schools, however, had no such restrictions and were free to roam at will through the town, the parents, no doubt, secure in the knowledge that none of our predatory boys lurked in the streets.

No doubt the four headmasters and headmistresses, who wielded absolute power both in and out of school, had come to the conclusion that the extension of segregation beyond the immediate precincts would ensure that there could not be any unforeseen or unfortunate consequences if excessive propinquity was denied.

But the vacations were not policed, and youth somehow found a way. Cinemas were out of bounds, and on one 'half' in the afternoon, when Bill Upcott Gill, the Head of Classics, and I went to see a film, we saw the bottoms of a group of boys as they left bent double, having only just arrived and paid for their seats. Others fled from the tennis club whenever we arrived towards lock-up time in the evening. After Saturday morning school, those attending for roll call who were not playing in a match had to attend for roll call on the first fifteen touchline or at the cricket field, where 'Windy' Gale or Millman, later to captain county sides respectively at Middlesex and Nottingham, dominated the square.

In those long post-war summers of the fifties the eight rowed in the regattas at Bedford, Henley and Marlow, the whole school (yes, the whole school except for non-swimmers) jumped into the Ouse and swam the half mile of the 'long swim' with the staff rowing amongst them to pull out those in distress. Non-swimmers. were few, and any who had not swum his pass of a half mile kept a white button on the top of his school headgear, which in those days looked like a Jewish skullcap and was worn at all times in the streets. The theory was that should anyone espy such an article floating on lake or river he could assume that the owner must be in distress nearby and act accordingly. Even as an assistant master it was made clear that I should as a matter of good example swim my pass as a non-swimmer. I managed to do so, but was not of course expected to wear the offending button on my hat.

The combined cadet force of some 600 boys marched through the town behind a 50-piece band and produced national service officers while the Empire slowly decayed. School chapel on Sunday mornings left us with little time of our own. Work was assiduously marked, and pay was miniscule. My Scholarship money at Oxford and pay as an army captain had both exceeded that of a newly-appointed master. 'An apprenticeship for a Headmastership' said Taylor. 'You'll need a gown and hood.' And incidentally the staff wear a dinner jacket at functions such as the boat club ball. But there was no pay cheque until well into the Michaelmas term, and £415 a year did not go very far even in those days to support a growing family.

But there was another side to the coin. Most boys had two parents, and Mother was at home when they arrived back from school. Schoolgirl pregnancies were practically unknown. Indeed eyebrows were raised if a boy was seen too frequently with a girl. There were no drugs on sale. Children read books, and video nasties had not been invented. Work was closely marked and monitored and most could spell.

There was, notwithstanding, a strong hierarchy in the schools, the universities and in society at large. Mediocre boys in my sixth form gained places at Oxbridge on the strength of the school's reputation and went up to read rugby or rowing. Closed scholarships or the parental purse were another ladder.

I cannot help feeling, in spite of having spent a very happy ten years teaching at a public day school, that there were not a few amongst our alumni who found themselves later in life rather out of their depth in shallow water. This I fear may not have a little to do with some of the problems of power leadership which face the country today. On the other hand schools are, at their best, the setters of standards and the upholders of much of what is best in English education. Long may they continue to be so. They are now much more aware of the dangers of being too much divorced from the broader sector of public education.

The common room in any school can develop a spiders-in-a-bottle syndrome, and schoolmasters can in some cases earn the jibe that they are men with boys and boys with men. BMS, although a very happy place, threw up its rivalries and jealousies. A pair of kippers left inadvertently in a man's pocket in the staff anteroom for several days was the touchpaper for a protracted row between the owner and a rival who discovered them that went on for days, during which wrongs and antipathies that had festered for years were aired in public. For months afterwards neither would stay in the same room with the other. But for myself it was with mixed feelings of sadness that I began to realise that a growing family of five needed more than the meagre salary of an assistant master, and although by now in charge of a department and head of the middle school, I was to be interviewed, now just in my early thirties, for the headmastership of half a dozen public and grammar schools. Soon I found a sympathetic governing body and was appointed the twentieth headmaster of the 350-year-old Wilson's Grammar School in Camberwell. It was to become a lifetime's labour of love, lubricated with a little more liberty. But again the paradox remained. On the other side of the coin were the shackles of responsibility.

CHAPTER THIRTEEN

HEADHUNTING
AND OTHER SPORTS

Philip Frenau wrote: 'What madness is ambition. To forfeit ease and that domestic bliss which is the lot of happy ignorance'. Many a young schoolmaster or mistress living a happy, penurious but contented life becomes seized by a fit of madness at *'un certain age'* to become the head of an institution. All this is very commendable, but the path ahead for the aspiring candidate is strewn with thorns, although such posts, especially in the inner cities, are less sought after today than the vacant headships of the more comfortable country grammar schools of yesteryear, which often attracted scores if not hundreds of applications. It was not uncommon for some candidates to apply for everything across the board, in an operation known as blanketing. After some early experience in the writing of forms of application the hopeful embryo head would get onto the 'circuit'. This was a sort of club of the better qualified and more likely aspirants, who would meet on trains or station platforms or in anterooms, from which one would disappear into his new office. Returning on the London train, after an unsuccessful interview for the headmastership of an attractive riverside town grammar school in Oxfordshire, we defeated candidates asked the new appointee his secret of success.

'Simple' he said. 'At my present public school we have compiled amongst us some 200 questions and answers. Try me.'

'You are at present a sixth form master at a boys' public school' one of our number began. 'How is your experience relevant to your seeking to be the head of a mixed country grammar school?'

Straight out came the answer. 'You say, 'I live in a matriarchal society at home with a wife and two daughters'. This gets them laughing and then you're away.'

Practice interviews with a tape recorder in front of a mirror had brought his expertise to a high pitch. Nowadays no doubt it would have been a video camera on a tripod.

We wished him luck, and secretly in our hearts wished the same to his new staff. In similar vein, it was always wise to avoid pomposity, that occupational disease which afflicts headmasters who after a time can come to confuse themselves with the deities.

Politics could be an equally dangerous trap for aspiring heads. An old friend and colleague applying for the headmastership of a grammar school in Lancashire was at a late stage undecided as to whether he wished to accept the post should it be offered to him. The penalty for too late a withdrawal could be a failure to pay his travel expenses. Up from the deep blue south, he looked round at the committee and decided that his best line of retreat lay in a final declaration. The Chairman asked him 'What are your interests outside the school in the general community?'

'I am a member of the Conservative Party' my friend declared. To his surprise there were smiles all round. He was appointed. He made an excellent headmaster of the local grammar school.

Racial discrimination could also rear its ugly head. When I had been shortlisted for the headmastership of Haverfordwest Grammar School and was travelling by train through the Principality on the way to the interview, a Welsh lady began weighing me up in the carriage. Finally her curiosity got the better of her. 'Will you be here then for the headmastership?' she asked, as we trundled through Pembrokeshire. I admitted as much. 'And which of the gentlemen will you be?' she asked, referring to the local paper she had been reading. It apparently contained an advance list of the candidates' names and backgrounds. I pondered upon what odds were being offered against me at the Joe Corals of those days in the fifties.

Later that day in Haverfordwest, twelve of us were interviewed by what we were told was a sub committee of about twenty people. We were informed that on the following day a short list of us would be summoned to the local courtroom, where we would be confronted by the whole education committee, the candidates appearing, we assumed, in the dock. It soon became clear that a number of Joneses, Evanses and Reeses were to be favoured. My own inclusion, I assumed, had been the result of being mistaken for a Welshman as a result of an education at Jesus College Oxford, which is an exclave of Wales.

Eventually an old boy of the school was appointed, and he became a most successful headmaster. The failed candidates debated at the hotel at dinner on the evening before the final interview as to whether they might seek admission to the court on the following morning in the public gallery and shout 'There were better men here yesterday!'

Sex could also rear its enticing head. Marius Rosa in his *Intelligent Teachers Guide to Preferment* quotes as follows:

Chairman: 'Er be a foine figure of a woman.'
Second Manager: 'Aah.'
Third Manager: 'Er be a *very* foine figure of a woman.'
Chairman (to Director of Education): 'Ave you seen 'er teach?'
Director: 'Yes, I've seen her take a PT class.'
Managers in unison: 'Aah. '
Second manager to vicar: 'If we appoint 'er, vicar, ye'll be down at school more often, won't ye?'
Vicar: 'She seemed to be a very suitable candidate. I shall do my best to help her if she comes.'
Chairman (reflectively): 'She be a very well-built woman, very well set on her feet.'

Rose also quotes another interview where a less well-informed governor of a school remarked 'BA, BA! We don't want to know if her's got a BA. Has her got Matric?'

There are other legendary stories of governors who thought an MA Cantab related to a degree conferred by the Archbishop of Canterbury. But a nodding acquaintance with the angels is still a useful qualification to gain preferment in the more distinguished schools.

Candidates for office can also show extreme nervousness. Rose quotes the case of a woman who was interviewed for the headship of a local primary school. Overcome by the oppressive atmosphere and the importance of the occasion, she fainted and had to be carried out of the room in a fireman's lift by the clerk to the governors, revealingly displaying her disarranged clothing. The effect on the next candidate waiting outside the door may well be imagined.

Eventually, when appointed, it becomes the responsibility of the new headmaster (at least in the school over which I presided) to make his own appointments. I had a similar unnerving experience to that recounted by Rose when appointing a librarian. The lady concerned, an Oxford graduate and rather overqualified for the job, arrived in an extremely nervous state. Doing my best to put her at ease, I offered her one of the two easy chairs in my study which stood side by side to accommodate the two parents which boys then invariably had. The lady concerned seized hold of the back of one chair. She then grabbed the back of the other one and sat down on the carpet, falling backwards to expose a pair of bright green knickers. After a fraught interview, she seized the doorknob but was unable to turn it. I tried to assist her, but her finger were tightly clamped round the knob. When I had prised them loose I was able to release her from her ordeal. She was not appointed.

An old friend, then headmaster of Haberdashers' Askes' School, recounted how he had received an application from a Mr Patel for a physics mastership. In the usual way, Frank wrote to the referees quoted on the candidate's curriculum vitae. A letter duly came back from one of them which said in so many words that Mr Patel was an absolutely first rate schoolmaster, a man of probity, distinction and with substantial experience with boys. He was all that any headmaster might require in a man for the post on offer. But there was, continued his referee, one matter of some possible weakness which he felt should be brought to the headmaster's attention, and that related to the level of his qualifications to teach the more advanced work to boys in the sixth form. The letter continued 'I, on the other hand, am well qualified to tackle this sort of challenge.' The headmaster appointed neither candidate.

Those seeking posts to teach mathematics and science were few and far between in the full employment of the post-war years. However, one of my predecessors, Bill Hecker, later Headmaster of St Dunstan's College, said that that in his day between the wars, if a physics post fell vacant, he and his wife would sit down on the carpet and throw all the applications from third, lower second class or Irish candidates on one side and then get down to compiling a short list from the rest. But in the new post-war climate in the fifties, deciding to teach was a form of economic masochism fired only by the hope that we were sowing the seeds of a future career of promotion and rapid advancement in education.

Richard Baker, the TV newsreader who I had known in my schooldays when his London Grammar school was evacuated to Northampton, served for a time as a member of the staff of the grammar school of which I was later to become Headmaster. On one occasion a pupil commiserated with him about the poor returns that schoolmasters were receiving in those early post-war days. 'My father is in the fruit trade' said the lad. 'Now if you'd like to join him in the business in the Walworth Road I'm sure he could offer you something more than they're giving you at the grammar school.'

Instead of accepting this well-meaning and generous offer, Richard went to the BBC, where I believe he made a rather better living for himself than he might have enjoyed as a barrow boy.

Upon receiving references about a candidate, it is often useful to have some knowledge of the writer. Headmasters know well the unscrupulous colleague who might deliver fulsome praise of a candidate of whom they wished to dispose. Equally unprofessional was the conduct of the poacher who, having heard of my superb secretary, covertly got in touch to make her an offer which she wisely refused.

The reference that read 'Mr John Smith was a master at this school from January 1969 to January 1970' told all; more is often to be read between the lines than within the content.

It is, I believe, the practice in the navy for an annual report on each officer to be seen, read and initialled by the individual concerned. A naval friend told me of such a report in which the captain said, quite baldly 'This officer uses my ship as a convenient means of transport from one assignation to another and is, moreover, often drunk.' The officer objected to the report and the captain agreed to make an alteration. The word 'assignation' was changed to 'port' and the report ended with the words 'moreover he is often sober'.

To return, however, to my own experience as a newly-appointed headmaster. Although at the time, aged 35, I looked to my disadvantage many years younger. Indeed, at a headmasters' conference at St Olaves Grammar school I was greeted by the then head of that institution as the senior prefect. This did not help when most of my new staff were rather older than myself. It was with some trepidation that I met many of them for the first time as I took morning prayers in the great hall. Several were late or chose not to attend. This did not augur well. But a good number of them were in attendance at the bar of the local Grove Tavern throughout a protracted lunch hour. It was quite clear that something had to be done. The battle for survival that ensued resulted in a number of casualties, including the resignations under duress of a psychopathic housemaster and one or two others who had been appointed during the barrel-scraping years of wartime staffing.

My predecessor, retiring in his 70th year, had lost much of his vigour. During the war the school had been evacuated to share premises with Christ's Hospital, the public school at Horsham, and this had taken its toll of his energies. Nor did staffing improve much as the university graduates of the 1960s entered the schools. The impact of the post-war years of full employment was felt no more acutely than in the inner city schools. The dead hand of the National Union of Teachers on salary policy meant that we could pay but a small differential to a sixth form physics master over that paid to the abundant supply of young women flooding into the primary schools to teach five-year-olds. The result was that many headmasters were forced to make appointments of staff way beyond the ceiling of those individuals' competence. Some were young hotheads who inhabited the infra-red end of the political spectrum, and some of these sought to undermine the stability of the institutions they had joined to serve. There were cries to do away with uniforms, put members of the sixth form on the governing bodies of the schools and members of the cleaning staff as well. Let all decisions, however small, be decided in endless committee by common consent.

The battles of the new liberalism were fought by headmasters throughout London. This I was to find out when I was to become the London Chairman of the Headmasters' Association. Consultation is a fine and necessary exercise, but spending most of one's time in the classroom and getting on with the job of teaching is more important.

But for myself, a measure of order was established with the help of the staff, many of whom were of pre-war vintage. There were enough wiser and older heads among them to clip the wings of the fledglings. Within a few weeks of taking office I found other allies in Her Majesty's Inspectorate and asked them to come and make a full inspection of the school. This was not entirely popular, but Headmasters must not count upon too much popularity. If you are liked by all and sundry when in any senior office, there may well be something wrong with you and the institution that you manage.

But later, as I looked around the faces of my staff at the beginning and end of term it was quite clear that schoolmastering is no sinecure. Tired and drawn in July, they would look physically different men in September. But at both ends of the spectrum were the workaholics and the idle. Amongst the latter and well known to their colleagues were one or two who regularly took National Health Service holidays. This happens in all walks of life, and it has occurred to me that there might be some sense in providing a bonus payment for those who never or rarely absent themselves from their place of work. The majority do their jobs conscientiously and well, many attending in spite of minor illness. But like the poor, the idle are always with us, relying on colleagues to cover for absence or incompetence.

It has been said that those who cannot do teach, and that those who cannot teach teach teachers. The profession, often its own worst enemy, has its fair share of casualties and one might go even further to say that those who can neither teach nor teach teachers finish up in the hands of the psychiatrists. But example is better than precept, and here it is perhaps instructive to refer to the obligations of office laid down when the school was founded in the year 1615. The Headmaster was abjured 'to teach good manners, submit himself to the Governor's directions willingly, not to let the school at his own charge, not practise medicine, not absent himself for more than thirty days in the year, render an account annually to the Governors having first deducted his own stipend and not to keep an ale house, gaming house nor frequent ill houses! It will be seen that I was to be denied many of the simple pleasures of life and such strictures, it will be appreciated, made things very difficult for me.

I was further required to be 'sound in religion, honest, virtuous and discreet and be of a wise and sober and loving disposition, diligent, sedulous, fit and learned, a Master of Arts and able to make Greek and Latin verses'. These qualifications were laid down in the Founder's Charter under the great seal of James the 1st in 1615. (see *A Short History of Wilson's School,* by D H Allport and N J Friskney).

It will be readily appreciated that such constrictions, if applied to those who hold similar office today, might soon result in their hasty departure. Fortunately for me, the ancient sanctions were not adhered to closely and I was consequently able to cling on to my job for 25 years. In the army there is an award for such devotion to duty known as the Long Service and Good Conduct medal. As all old soldiers know, this is the reward for long years of undetected crime.

The boys for their part were required, amongst other things, to provide a testament, psalm book, paper, pens, ink, satchel, candles for use in winter, and to be clean and healthful in body, properly clothed, not to bring pocket money to school and to pay the Master's dues on admission and tuppence every quarter towards brooms and rods. The birch broom was by now out of fashion, but the rod was in full swing. The prefects also administered corporal punishment. This had to be stopped, and in this I had the full support of the previous year's Captain of School, a most charming young man, who was awaiting the start of the term at the University, where he later gained a distinguished first. His name was Bryan Masters, and he is now an eminent and successful writer who, with other old boys such as Roy Porter, has made his name in the world of letters. He offered his help to the new headmaster pending his going up to University. I thanked him politely and told him that I'd rather get on with the job in my own way.

But apart from problems of staffing and discipline, there were other difficulties. Back in Camberwell after the war and relocated in its ancient premises, the school was finding the recruitment of suitable able pupils through the eleven-plus examination increasingly difficult. The catchment area had deteriorated. The Victorian buildings were out of date and crowded within narrow streets of houses owned by the trust which in part financed the school. With these, its function was to process able lads, many of working-class backgrounds, into middle-class citizens and export them to the outer suburbs. But a more serious problem was soon to rear its head. In 1965 the Labour Government of the day decided to kick the ladder from under the feet of the able children of humble origins in the inner cities. Afraid of tackling the real seat of privilege in the fee-paying sector, the Government published its circular number 10 of the year 1965. This circular was to be noted, appropriately, as the last year of British freedom. It presaged the move towards the establishment of a system of comprehensive education and the disappearance of the grammar schools. As I was by this time Chairman of the Headmasters' Association in London, I went with a lobby of headmasters to meet the Conservative education committee, then in opposition at the House of Commons. But our efforts were to no avail. Although at the time out of office, when returning to power later they were of little help. The political tide of the times had flowed too swiftly for all but the strongest swimmers to survive the move towards the new system. The voluntary schools, of which we were one, had the best chance of survival, so a small group of us entertained Margaret Thatcher to lunch. She spoke eloquently of her aversion to the things that were going on in the primary schools, where as she said, children were wasting time doing such things as making models of the Eiffel Tower out of Shredded Wheat packets and time wasting follies of like nature.

As I listened to her my mind wandered back to those long summer afternoons at the village school when the box of clay had been once again been brought out and yesterday's efforts squeezed back into smelly and sweaty balls for new creations to take shape, and the wasted hours of double digging in the Chairman of Governors' garden. I wondered whether our guest had had a like experience in Grantham, perhaps making raffia mats like the girls of our village. One thing was certain - that education had not greatly changed at that level.

She quoted a piece of doggerel that began: 'There's really nothing wrong with Roger, Mrs Proger' and went on to allay the concern of the parent that her son's inclination to show a deep interest in matters mathematical and scientific were quite normal for a child of eight. But in spite of this, neither as Secretary of State for Education nor later as Prime Minister was she able or politically prepared to oppose the movement towards a system which, in our eyes at the time, and more so today, was seen to be in some measure discredited. Speaking at a debate in Sidcup in this controversial matter, I suggested that it might be wiser to make butter for the sake of all the consumers if the cream was not put into the churn with the rest of the milk. The motion was, however, eloquently defended by Roy Hattersley and I had only a small handful of supporters. So it was that there began a great dispersal of the ancient grammar schools which had done so much for education in inner London.

St Olive's led the way to Bromley. We followed to the London Borough of Sutton. Amongst others Emanuel, Colfes, Owen's, wealthy foundations supported by livery companies sought salvation elsewhere, often as newly emerging public schools. Our local sister girls' school, Mary Datchelor, left it all too late and in spite of my own good offices at Sutton, where my old Oxford friend Harry Evans was Chief Education Officer, a great school had to close. The ladder for the working-class boy or girl into the professions which the grammar schools had provided was finally kicked away from under their feet by the government of the day, with little help from the opposition. We did our best, but only the better-founded schools survived. Our colleagues in the independent schools were more fortunate. Legislation to veto the right of parents financially to such schools is notoriously difficult to draft and would if successful lead to a diaspora to enclaves of freedom in the Channel Islands, Eire and the nearer continent. We can imagine the sort of things that might ensue:

Police Constable: 'I put my ear to the keyhole your worship and I heard the words 'mensa mensa mensam' being intoned by the defendant. Upon forcing an entry I found him alone in a room with two schoolboys conducting a class of instruction in a foreign language. Upon making further enquiries I found that he was engaging in this practice for remuneration. I thereupon charged him and placed him under arrest in accordance with the Education Control and Restriction Act'.

A brave new world indeed! The paradox in that last sad decade of the sixties was that precisely in those parts of rural England where comprehensive education had the best chance of success, local politics enabled the grammar schools to survive, while in the inner cities where the selective system had enabled the bright lad from a humble background to move ahead amongst his peers, the grammar schools became anathema to the local politicians. But those of us who held out still felt that we had done the right thing by our schools.

A story current at that time was of a headmaster presenting himself at the Pearly Gates and to his surprise finding himself greeted by the devil. 'Oh dear' said he. 'Have I come to the wrong place?'

'No, not at all' came the reply. 'Come in, we've just gone comprehensive.'

There were many of us who still felt that in an increasingly international league it would never be to the advantage of either the Arsenal or Puddlecombe Rovers to play in the same league, any more than it was for the very able and for those of low ability to be educated in the same school.

So it was to be that the Pearly Gates opened for us among the leafy lanes of the London borough of Sutton. The decision to move the ancient foundation was not taken lightly after three and a half centuries in Camberwell, and the complexities of moving a whole school, lock stock and barrel, together with its pupils, was daunting. The political, financial, legal and logistical problems were manifold. There was moreover a deal of ill-informed opposition to be faced and persuaded of the good sense of our decision.

Eight years of hard work with architects, planners, lawyers, local and national politicians and authorities were to follow.

Each of the voluntary schools which moved in this diaspora faced different but similar problems. But for myself, a moment of choice had again arrived. The seven-year itch of headmastering was upon me. Should I stay or move on? At just over forty, the time was ripe for fresh woods and pastures to be explored. Amongst others I asked a good friend, an old boy of the school who was a governor and a millionaire property man, for a reference. He was one of at least three old boys who had become rich at that time. His name was Bert Bourner. Another man who had made a million and who had also been supportive of his old school was Jim Maybank. The other well-known tycoon was the actor Michael Caine. He had not enjoyed his time at the school.

Bert Bourner had made his fortune in the post-war property boom. A man of enormous generosity, he owned a manor in Sussex, a private cinema in an adapted oast house, his own cricket ground and a passenger-carrying miniature railway some two miles long with three stations, each equipped with a bar. Each year he would host a party for scores of friends of the school at his home and serve a fine luncheon and tea in marquees. The guests would enjoy a match on his square, ride the railway and see the latest films in the cinema in the evening. On the occasion of the school's 350th anniversary celebrations, he invited the all the boys and parents to the estate and provided a fine lunch with vintage wines, strawberry tea and an ox roast in the evening. All this was accompanied by a match on the square between the school and the old boys whilst the local Edenbridge Silver Band played. It was not quite a feeding of the five thousand, but at least a thousand were royally fed and watered. In the meantime the railway, Bert driving the train, ran the guests round the estate, stopping at the stations, where Pimms was served in unlimited quantities.

Bert and I became close friends in those early years of headmastering. After governors' meetings, held at that time at his offices in St James, he and I would go to Quaglino's, in which he held an interest. He owned a number of cars, including Rolls Royces and a Bentley. One evening after a particularly good dinner I was asked which car we had with us. It had by this time become quite an unthinking reflex for me to say 'I'm not sure whether we've got the Rolls or the Bentley with us tonight'.

My world was changing. Alf, Bert's chauffeur, would drive us home as we sipped brandy from the cut-glass decanters in the back. He gave generously to the school, but both he and Rosalind, his wife, were to die before we opened the new buildings in Sutton.

In the meantime, in spite of a taste for high living, my own family finances were low and I decided to chance my luck at two or three public schools then advertising vacant headmasterships. I was soon called for interview at the oldest one in the country, at St Albans. Neither Kathleen nor I liked the headmaster's house, overlooked as it was by the common room. At Alleyn's, a joint foundation with Dulwich College, I was given a good blooding at the Grosvenor Hotel by Sir Hartley Shawcross, who had prosecuted in the war criminals' trials at Nuremberg. As he grilled me I felt for the one and only time a fleeting sympathy for them. But Charlie Lloyd got the job and later moved within the foundation to the Mastership of Dulwich College. Hearing of these shenanigans, Bert rang and asked me up to lunch in town at Quaglino's. He suggested that he and the other governors would like me to stay and move the school to its new home in Sutton. He made it clear that this could be both fascinating and rewarding. Planning and moving the ancient foundation would provide an exciting and absorbing challenge, one at least as interesting as taking on one of the independent schools which now seemed a logical career step ahead. I went home, wrote to the City of London school saying I would not now wish to be interviewed, and decided to stay. I never regretted it.

CHAPTER FOURTEEN

PUPILS, PARENTS
AND PRANKS

In Camberwell life had never lacked interest and stimulus. 'You've got a tea leaf in the school, and 'e's been telling you porky pies', said Miss Roberts. I looked at her questioningly. The quick South London intelligence rapidly grasped that the new Headmaster needed translation from the vernacular. It was a different language from the East Midland dialect which I knew so much better. All those years ago at the village school when Violet Wilkins had seen her four-year-old playing outside in the gutter and had shouted, 'Come on up orf aht on it'. Surely the longest possible string of prepositions possible, but I had understood immediately. Cockney rhyming slang had been outside my experience. Correction of speech was constant, but graffiti were never tolerated.

I saw some of the best examples of that art in a well-known ladies' college in the south west when I attended a conference of headmasters and headmistresses there whilst the Head of a famous girls' school told me in later years that the choicest language was generated by her more aristocratic pupils. Little ever came to my ears in Camberwell, but the tea leaves often needed stirring and the porky pies sniffed with suspicion.

Two brothers, bright boys, had absented themselves from

school. With no customary parental letter of excuse, I asked the parents to visit. "'e's dahn the station answering questions' said father. 'We only went away for a few days to his auntie's funeral. I can't believe it. They broke into a shop. Little devils, after all we've done to bring them up properly and honest. Nothing like this has ever been known to happen in the family before.'

I suggested they might seek to complete their education elsewhere rather than suffer the stigma of expulsion. As father left the building, a senior master stopped me. 'Didn't you know that that man is one of the best known fences in South London?' he said. He could have fooled me.

Other absentees in September before the advent of hop-picking machinery were rumoured to be on holiday in Kent, and to my chagrin able boys of 15 would from time to time be withdrawn from school because 'His uncle's got a place for him in the print'. Trade union protected sinecures were well paid in those days. We were entertained by many colourful characters, amongst the parents, ranging from the Camberwell Beauty, wife of a well-known all-in wrestler, who would attend in full leopard-skin gear, to a mum of blatantly provocative sexuality who sought an interview to complain that her telephone number was being advertised at a number of main-line London railway stations and that she was receiving numerous calls that her son's favours were for sale. I suggested that she approach the police, as the authorities most appropriately able to deal with this matter. But I began to wonder, as she edged her chair closer to mine and leaned forward to whisper confidentially that only that morning she had had a caller who said that what she needed herself was a 'good stiff prick'.

Such were the hazards of headmastering in Camberwell.

Life was never dull. The boys were loyal and hard working and the parents delighted and often astonished, as their geese really did turn out to be swans and flew away on white wings to the universities to become dons, doctors, lawyers, bankers or civil servants. The bank balance of gratitude was great and a constantly-welcomed reward for our labours. Parental discipline was strong and there were few divorces. The bizarre case of a parent, however, who beat his son with a television aerial and his wife if the vegetables were not located in the correct quadrant of his dinner plate, although meriting the ministrations of Dr Sachs, were the exception rather than the rule. When I bought the church and church hall at Talybont on Usk in Breconshire to provide a field studies centre, there were boys who thought that the bumps of the Brecons were the next best thing to Everest. The goodwill we enjoyed was enormous. All this was to go. The geese of Camberwell, who to the delight of many parents turned out to be swans, were to be replaced by just a few of the swans of Sutton, who, to the disappointment of their parents, were really geese. Warrens and Waynes were replaced by Olivers and Jonathans. Camberwell needed its grammar school, but not as part of a comprehensive nonsense on several sites. It was with mixed feelings of sadness for the future of those we could no longer serve that we left for the leafy lanes of Surrey.

There followed a period during which we first bussed boys into town from the sunny suburbs and then, when in the new school, in the opposite direction. These were difficult days, but of great interest. Academically the inner city boys were very numerate, but their literacy often left a good deal to be desired. Mathematics is the *lingua franca* of intelligence. Literacy, first learned at home, was at more of a discount with some. Foreign languages turned out to be their greatest problem. Our new pupils from the gin-and-Jaguar belt, whilst equally numerate, were also more literate in the main, whilst foreign travel had lent a reality to foreign languages. So as the school settled down in its new role, we steadily built up the standards of scholarship and university placement to those to which I had been accustomed in my days at Bedford Modern School. The predominantly middle-class parents of Sutton, however, had offspring who often compounded more sophistication in their misdeeds than their working class Camberwell contemporaries. Complaints came to me that some boys, particularly in the afternoon, were not quite so alert as they were during the morning session. This is not an uncommon failing with boys, and indeed with schoolmasters. It was also reported that the breath of some members of the sixth form was less pleasant after lunch. Drifts of information from one or two parents suggested that sugar was disappearing from kitchens at home in unusually large quantities, and during a routine check in the locker rooms a quantity of yeast was found. The illicit brewery was eventually uncovered in a disused caretaker's lavatory. I did not inform the governors of the day that inadvertently I had had charge of an alehouse, but I gathered that the beer was of acceptable quality.

Nowadays when I attend old boys' dinners it is clear that their education was not entirely a waste of time, although as I listen to some of the speeches I am reminded of the advice given by a furniture restorer that a little alcohol can soon remove the polish from a veneer. Schoolmasters as well as boys can be less attentive to their duties in the long summer afternoons. Members of the mathematical sixth form decided on one occasion that the tedium of the last period on Friday afternoon might be conveniently shortened. It is customary in most academic institutions for the day to be punctuated by a bell or a buzzer. This the boys carefully recorded on tape. Some twenty minutes before the appointed end of the afternoon, the button was pressed by a boy in the back row of the class and the terminal pips rang out to mark the appointed end of the day. Absent-mindedly the master dismissed the class, which had long since dispersed by the time he reached the common room and saw the clock.

There can be confusion with the season of the year as well as the time of day. J Clark in his delightful book *The Inspector Remembers* tells of two neighbouring village schools where the headmasters were covenanted to communicate a warning to one another should one of these unwelcome gentlemen arrive on their premises. They had in addition arranged an agreed code in order that the pupils should be unaware of headmasterly collusion.

One bright day in autumn, the visitor reached one of the schools and a senior boy was despatched post haste across the fields to warn the neighbours of the enemy at the gate. Unfortunately the inspector in pony and trap arrived at the other academy at about the same time as a red-faced and bucolic boy burst into the headmaster's room and delivered his message: 'The cuckoo has arrived early this spring!'

At the interfaces which lie between family and school, between parent and child, the adult and the young in constant contact, there is always a potential for half understanding. At this frontier between youth and age there can often be found a latent source of potential humour. For without a sense of humour, the schoolmaster or schoolmistress can be lost, whilst with it, all things are possible. It has been well said that the family that plays together stays together. It might equally be said that the teacher and class which laugh together work well together. And thrice blessed is the teacher who can laugh at himself. From the beginning of the school day to the end there were times when, even at solemn moments, it was difficult to retain a sense of the serious side of life.

One morning at prayers in the great hall, having entered in gowned procession with the staff and prefects, I caught the eye of a boy well known for his mischievous nature. He had recently been reproved for a minor offence, having arrived at school in an untidy and dishevelled condition and flouting a minor dress regulation. As the organ began to play for the hymn, a breeze from an open door blew my gown across my trousers and a half smile lit up his face. It was then that I became aware that my flies were agape.

The spark of recognition which connected us throughout the Chaplain's morning address and the remainder of the service made it as difficult for me to contain my suppressed laughter as it was for him to contain his. But there are times when laughter has to be contained. How much easier it is when it can be released, such as on another morning after prayers when I announced how successful we had been in collecting a substantial sum to provide 'a blind dog for the guides'.

But often enough the pupil is the subject of the humour rather than the perpetrator. It is sound practice for headmasters to get out into the school each day and be seen frequently by boys and staff. The 'jack in office' syndrome is one to be avoided at all costs.

One day, having sent for a boy, I was called away into another part of the school and on returning to my study found him waiting outside. He had, apparently, knocked on my door with no response. Deciding that I might be inside but otherwise engaged, he had applied his eye to the keyhole. I crept up quietly behind him and tapped him on the shoulder.

'Have you seen anything good in there, Robbins?' I asked him. The robin's colour rose up from his breast, through his neck and up to his scalp. 'No sir' he gulped. Then we both had our chuckle. There are those very few occasions when the *mot juste* happily springs to mind.

Another time, during what my own headmaster at Bedford Modern used to describe as his 'archidedactical perambulations', I espied a boy in the locker room scratching around on hands and knees when he should have been in class. 'What is this boy, why are you not in your class?' I snapped.

'Please sir, I am looking for my inflexible ruler' he stuttered.

'He stands before you!' I replied. 'Return to your class, for you have indeed found him'.

Locker rooms and lavatories are places in schools which must needs be watched by authority. Posting graffiti was always regarded as a heinous offence meriting mass expiation by detention. The result was that the scribbling of fools was rarely seen. On one occasion the whole school remained behind until the culprit acknowledged that he had written on a lavatory wall 'If you can read this you are sitting the wrong way round.' But as F E Smith once remarked, one of the advantages of universal education is that the writing on the lavatory wall appears lower down year by year.

Another locker room offence came to light when a boy attended the medical room with blackened finger nails. It was only some time later when I heard that a member of the sixth form had been suffering from frequent raids on packets of biscuits that he kept in the dark recesses of his locker that I was able to gather the cause of his colleague's injury. A resourceful lad, he had carefully baited a large mousetrap in the dark recesses at the back of his locker. There were no more thefts. Patrolling the premises on another day, a boy who was late for his class shot around the corner and ran into his headmaster with considerable force. We both stood shocked for a moment, and then he cried 'Oh my god!'

'Yes my boy, but incognito at present' came my reply.

Some Headmasters do indeed find themselves imprinted with the paternalism born of long holding office and the occupational disease from which many suffer is pomposity.

But for serious offences against the community, there must always be punishment. During my 25 years as a headmaster the use of the cane gradually diminished. There was also the odd occasion when a miscarriage of justice took place. But then it was sufficient to point out that no doubt it could be interpreted as retribution for the many times on which he had not been found out. This was cheerfully accepted.

There was indeed much to be said for letting the punishment fit the crime. One lad, on finding himself in detention writing an essay on 'My ideal school', suggested that such an institution should contain an 'anger room' provided with punch bags and boxing gloves to allow boys to vent their spleen to relieve pressures felt for injustices done by fellow pupils, masters and others. I suggested to him that the squash courts and football field provided that requirement.

A rather briefer essay was the result of a visit by Somerset Maugham to his old school to present the prizes. He arrived early in the day and was asked by the headmaster to talk to the sixth form on any topic he chose. The great man decided to talk about the construction of the short story. Each story, he suggested, should ideally contain four themes.

'You should use these as a sort of peg on which to hang your literary hat' he said. 'There should be some religious content, some reference to class, some to sex and last an air of mystery.'

After speech day was over the headmaster decided to let his sixth form have a try. Upon looking over the scripts he was to find one more concise than the rest, indeed confined to the single sentence 'My God!' said the Duchess. 'I'm pregnant. Who done it?'

The headmaster, a wise man, congratulated him upon his effort. In the same way a tempered reproof can often be better received and taken and be more effective than a direct one. Dylan Thomas recounted how he was seen out of school one day by his headmaster. He was a busy man and the matter slipped his mind. After a few days the application of a direct disciplinary sanction seemed to be too retrospective. As he passed Thomas in the corridor he stopped briefly and remarked 'Oh, I believe you were out of school when I was at the bank the other day. It's a good job nobody saw you'.

The unconscious humour that lies at the interface between age and youth is seen in even sharper relief in the primary schools. Mrs Robinson was a local teacher who wore deep cut V-necked sweaters and was rather well developed in the upper parts of her anatomy. One small boy complained to his mother that he didn't really like her. 'Why so?' asked his mother. 'Mrs Robinson is a very nice lady.' To which David replied, 'I don't like it when she bends over me in class because then I can see her lungs.'

Then there was the small girl just learning to write. 'What did you do at school today?' asked her mother?

'Oh', came the answer. 'We learned how to make babies.'

Somewhat surprised at such an answer from a six-year-old, her mother probed further. 'How do you do it?' she asked. 'It's easy' replied Helen. 'You just change the 'y' into 'ies'.

Another bright spark at the evening meal with guests at the table enquired of her parents 'Do you and daddy have sexual relations?' Her mother, somewhat nonplussed, said' Why do you ask darling?'

'Well', came the answer, 'if you do, do I know any of them?'

Or there is that probably apocryphal story of the father leaving for a dinner party who was asked by a young member of his family why he was wearing that funny black bow tie and suit.

'Why do you ask?' said daddy.

'You know it always makes you feel ill in the morning' replied the child.

A more penetrating and chilling enquiry about ultimate things came from another small child showing the concern that comes to us all at an early age about our final destination. 'When we die and go to heaven, do we go to Heathrow or Gatwick?' she asked.

Each year it fell to my lot to interview some hundreds of boys and parents for the 120 places at the school from amongst those who had passed the entrance examination. The mechanics of this required a brief word with parents and boy, a talk alone with the prospective pupil, who would read a passage from a book, talk about it and answer a few bland but often revealing questions about interests, games and hobbies, and why he wanted to come to the school. The boy would then be asked to leave and a few parting words would be spoken between the headmaster and parent. This is the practice in most schools which enjoy a measure of independence. Having completed this procedure with one family, my secretary came in with coffee at mid morning to say that a boy who had been interviewed at 9.30 had completely disappeared, and in spite of a thorough search of the premises was nowhere to be found.

It so happened that there were three doors into my study. One gave access to the school, another to my secretary and a third to a small lavatory. Bent down over my desk to write notes about the last candidate, I had asked him to wait outside. He had unfortunately left by the wrong door and had dutifully stood by the lavatory pan for much of the rest of the morning. He later proved to be a most diligent and obedient pupil.

And so we continued to examine and interview. This was not always without some humour. One morning a mother accompanied her offspring into my study and as she sat down she looked me straight in the eye and gave a broad and deliberate wink. She was not unattractive.

As she left at the end of the session, she repeated the exercise, smiling in a 'come hither' manner. My secretary, who had ushered her in, noticed these covert invitations, if indeed that is what they were, and remarked (for she was ever discreet), 'Did you see that last parent? She had a nervous tic.'

I pondered upon the greater temptations of one or two friends in the medical profession, who unlike headmasters were bound by a Hippocratic oath, but resisting temptation did not admit the boy. Speaking later of this to Brian Dance, a friend who was at the time the Headmaster of St Dunstan's College, a nearby public school, he told me 'I had a much more exciting experience. During the interview season last year I had a mother who attended my study wearing a blouse cut so low that her upper endowment was so substantially exposed that her cup was running over'. As this woman left Bryan's study she walked up to his desk, placed both hands upon it and bent low over it. The soft rock of ages was visibly cleft for the headmaster as she said in the most husky voice imaginable 'Mr Dance, I'd do anything to get my boy into the college'.

At a university dinner I recounted these anecdotes to the headmistress of a girls' public school, who told me that she too had been approached. This time it was a father who had remained in her study, the daughter having departed. Upon getting up to leave the room he dropped a bundle of bank notes on the carpet, tightly held together by a rubber band. Hurriedly she sent for her secretary, who followed him as he left the building to return them. The girl was not admitted.

At the top end of the school, headmasters in the sixties were much exercised by the virus of discontent that stemmed from the universities, the nascent pop culture and adolescent discontent of that unfortunate period of so called liberalism when many interpreted liberty as licence. One of the unhappy results of the times in which we live is the earlier age at which the young are deemed to reach years of discretion.

We all live that much longer, and it seems a pity to hasten too soon out of our childhood and then into adolescence and young adulthood. Much might be gained if the young were not subject to such intense social pressures and were able to enjoy longer the years of innocence and awaken later to the harsher realities of the world. These pressures become more intense as we move towards the inner cities and down the ladder of the class structure. Like Shakespeare's shepherd in *Winters Tale*, there were times when we thought 'I would that there were no age between sixteen and three-and-twenty or that youth would sleep out the rest'.

At four score years and one today
You're deemed to be discreet
To go in pubs and sit upon
A parliamentary seat.
See naughty films or go to jail
And leave the family nest
Or back a horse and lose your all
Right down to shirt and vest.

For Shakespeare in the Winter's Tale
Tells us with every care
To watch our fathers and pay heed
To wisdom and grey hair.
So woe betide the wayward wight
Who reaches one and twenty
To find that in the years between
The old man has learned plenty.

But this is sadly out of date, and we see eighteen or even sixteen as years of discretion. There were many I met at old boys' dinners who agreed with Mark Twain that 'when I was eighteen I thought my father knew nothing, but by the time I had reached twenty-one I was astonished how much the old man had learned in three years'. But most of our pupils seemed grateful, and few I believe would have agreed with that other cynic George Bernard Shaw that their education was interrupted schooling.

CHAPTER FIFTEEN

STAYING A HEAD

For fifteen years the mullioned windows of my study in the ancient grammar school had looked out on the busy streets of south London. Now a picture window looking onto the broad acres of the playing fields on the edge of the green belt was my new perspective. The architects had done their worst. Few clients are on the best of terms with their architects after eight years. The gas pipes in one of the advanced physics laboratories had ejected hot water and the swimming pool leaked. But despite of a few deficiencies, Sir Richard Shepherd's firm had designed well within a limited budget. As I looked through the window and watched the boys laughing and talking on the way to the tuck shop, from a few hundred yards away near the Cadet Force there came a loud explosion. Quickly running out across the first eleven square, gown blowing in the wind, I rapidly scattered a group of candidates for a lunchtime disciplinary enquiry. The prefect on duty had, however arrived first and spotted his man. Within the hour a parent was summoned to the school and a discussion ensued about sugar, fertiliser and biro pen tops packed with the lethal cocktail. Dire warnings followed of possible expulsion and there were promises of 'It will never happen again Headmaster, I can assure you'.

The quality of mercy is self-retrospection. I had always found explosives interesting. My thoughts went back to the Officers' Training Corps at Oxford and a first opportunity to command a troop of twenty-five pounders at Churn camp. 'Troop target HE 117 Charge three zero five five degrees angle of sight one zero minutes elevation three six hundred FIRE!' The crack of the gun would sound and a few seconds later the explosion, on a target way beyond Carshalton Beeches. Hopefully a lucky hit on the offices of the Local Education Authority, which had been particularly tiresome of late. Another sip of cold coffee and thoughts further back upon a day a lifetime away.

Tubby Clark had sat at the next desk to me at the grammar school in those far off days in the thirties and lived over a small corner shop in Collingwood road, Northampton. Such businesses dotted the streets of most small towns in the years between the wars, yielding a bare competence to their owners. November the fifth was an unusually difficult time for those who stocked fireworks. There were always a few left over, and in the damp of Pa Clark's unheated premises there was little hope that the remnants would last until next year. So a few sixpenny rockets and halfpenny bangers became our perquisites. These, together with a handful of rubber bands, a bottle and the careful alignment with the touch papers in close proximity, made hazardous and unpredictable missiles. Our imaginary enemies, who we were later to meet in more lethal encounters, lay across the Channel, but this was out of range of our juvenile artillery. In the village where we lived, which lay a few miles away from the town, Tubby would visit us for tea on Saturdays. Across the road from our cottage was the yard of a local pub and as the Saturday night singers left the bar we took careful aim. Troop target, HE 117 Charge 3 angle of sight... but we never got it quite right. We were never caught. We deserved to be.

The quality of mercy is an uneasy conscience. 'Yes Headmaster, he must never do it again, most reprehensible. I cannot think what came over him. Never in our experience at home has he ever done anything like this before. Thank you Headmaster, ! will guarantee that he will never do such a thing again in future.'

Spare thou them that confess their faults and restore thou them that are penitent. I pondered upon what I might say in prayers next morning. Oh, how original is sin. How important to discourage les autres. What, I tried to recall, had my own Headmaster said at Northampton Grammar School all those years ago when Ralph Hudson, who was later to be my best man, had put nitrogen iodide in the chalk. When Taffy Davis, Head of Physics, applied it to the blackboard that memorable morning, there had been some very interesting crackles and scatters as it exploded and fragmented. Fortunately Ralph was soon to escape with an open award at Merton College Oxford, whilst he and I as an Exhibitioner at nearby Jesus left behind us childish things. Ralph's next association with chalk was to be his work with the Chalk River project in Canada later in the war, when he helped in the production of the atomic bomb and later still as Professor of Nuclear Physics at the University of Illinois.

Another sip of the cold coffee. Perhaps our later achievements in this world help us to expiate our sins. But nonsense. This will not do. Boys are barbarians. They need civilising. Other reminiscences of days spent later in the war on the rocket anti-aircraft battery in Liverpool as a young subaltern and later as an infantry officer in the 8th Army when we were no longer needed in anti-aircraft defence at home. But that was different. We had a licence to kill and had been merciful when we were able. And next week was November 11th and the wreath laying on the school war memorial. I must give it more thought this evening at home.

Morning break is over as the telephone rings and I dive back from muddled reminiscence into the whirlpool of the day. Perhaps we never really grow up. Men with boys, boys with men. I meet a new first-form boy in the corridor. It is lunch time and he asks me if I could lend him ten pence. I know what it is for. We have a corridor telephone which they can use.

'I hope you're not telephoning your bookmaker to place bets at Epsom' I say. The small boy looks astonished that this begowned authority, whose word, as far as he is concerned, is law, could possibly imagine that he would do such a thing, let alone have the effrontery to ask the Headmaster to finance it.

'No sir, to ring my mother.'

As I walk away I wonder what he will say to her over the dinner table tonight.

April the first arrives and I announce from the platform that the school day is to be extended by an hour. The shock wave murmurs through the great hall until I remind them of the date. But next year the prefects have their revenge, and just before I am due to make my daily entrance in cap and gown a bogus double beats me to it. Dressed in an identical grey pinstripe with a duplicate of the tie I have been wearing for weeks, in a tattered MA gown borrowed from the common room, he proceeds to give out outrageous notices. And so we all remain children at heart. What pleasure it is to have such fun in the employment for which we are paid. Each day has the delights and sometimes the sorrows of a new situation.

Mr Chips knocks at my door. Many of the problems of the job derive from the common room. Thank goodness for Chips. A good headmaster should be in continual assessment of the changing abilities, efforts and potential of his staff, encouraging, advising and gently or otherwise reproving if necessary. Nowhere was I aware that this was so than as an examiner for the Cambridge University Examinations Syndicate. With experience it became increasingly clear that we were marking teachers and even schools as well as candidates. Sometimes it was not unknown to find currency or notes slipped between scripts from South East Asia, and even passionate pleas that 'I am the sole supporter of a widowed mother and several brothers and sisters and failure in this examination will entail poverty and deprivation for my family.' One fellow examiner even had a warning of intended suicide upon failure.

Schoolmasters, like people in every profession, come in all shapes and sizes. Down the centuries, from the village schoolmaster of Oliver Goldsmith's Deserted Village, whose parishioners wondered that his one small head could carry all he knew, through the wide range of those who laboured with no more than chalk and talk whilst their pupils dutifully plied their copies in slate pencils (which I did indeed myself at the village school). Then through the nineteenth century, schools as widely contrasting as the fictional Dotheboys Hall of Charles Dickens and the early enlightenment of Arnold of Rugby were to exhibit a gross polarity that was only to narrow into something more respectable in our own century, as public education developed. As the worst excrescences disappeared, the curriculum remained locked fast in the classics, with some lesser respectability accorded to Mathematics and History. Little else in the traditional schools of the Victorians mattered. Perhaps some of the problems of our country this century stem from this limited nourishment that those in power still drew from the roots of their education.

Headmasters are but schoolmasters writ large, and regrettably in not a few instances writ small. As in all walks of life, there are those who follow too much the devices and desires of their own hearts and stray from their ways like lost sheep, whilst some, like Lloyd George, turn out to be lost rams. But it would be wrong to assume that the great majority who teach in our schools are not hard working and dedicated and that in many cases they do not still treat the job as a vocation and a privilege. Mr Chips is still with us.

In the difficult days of staffing in the inner city areas in the time of full employment there were special problems. In the days of the unlamented Inner London Education Authority, an officer of that august body was charged with the responsibility of advising heads of schools and governors of the deficiencies of the more dubious characters who made a pathetic but sometimes predatory living on the fringes of the teaching profession. It came to the notice of a headmaster friend of mine at another grammar school that a part-time member of his staff who shared duties with a man in a similar part-time capacity at my own school was frequently absent from his classes. I had noticed the same pattern of sickness leave. I mentioned this to my Vice Chairman of Governors at a Rotary lunch one week and he asked me for the man's name. When I told him he drew in his breath.

'I know that man' said he. 'He is employed by me to run our youth centre in a full time capacity, but has been frequently away during the day on various pretexts. He wears a cassock and claims to hold a university degree.'

This had never been part of his CV when I had appointed him to teach physical education. He was consequently called up to face the three employers between whose institutions he had been juggling his services. On further probing about his qualifications it emerged that the degree he claimed had been awarded by an American university, but on being asked for its name he regretted that it had slipped his mind. We then discovered that his delayed arrival at the start of term had been the result of his driving lorries at a china clay works in Cornwall and not for a common cold. We all dispensed with his services forthwith, only to hear later that although informed of his misdemeanours, the Inner London Education Authority had now employed him as a teacher on the other side of town. I mention this simply as an illustration of how desperate was the shortage of teachers in those hard times.

But there were other offenders of a more scandalous and even criminal nature. A chemistry master at a South London Comprehensive school was found to have been dealing with chemicals of a more deadly nature in his laboratories than those usually associated with the instruction of the young, and he tried to derail a train with his lethal cocktail at St Mary Cray in South London. As an IRA activist, he went to prison. At another South London grammar school, a certain member of the staff was inclined to talk freely about his domestic life. A colleague in the common room took careful note of his indiscretions, including details of how he had copulated with a Woolworth's assistant whilst taking cover under the counter during an air raid in the war. This he contrasted with intercourse with his wife, which he said had been 'like getting into bed with a shark'. Upon leaving the grammar school and obtaining promotion to a senior post in a provincial town, the older man wrote to his former colleague saying that he had written a play which was about to be staged at a local theatre and that some of the characters were 'larger than life'. Armed with complimentary tickets, the unsuspecting victim went with his wife to see the first performance. when the curtain went up his wife let out a sigh of horrified anger as she saw the set on stage, which was decorated and furnished in the style of her own sitting room, and then proceeded to hear in the lines some of her own remarks and those of her husband, including those already mentioned. The play was taken off and a settlement was made out of court.

Headmasters and headmistresses are not immune from folly or scandal. One of the more celebrated of these involved the headmaster of a public school in the Midlands, who appointed an attractive young lady as matron and installed her in the staff accommodation provided on the opposite side of the quadrangle from the Headmaster's house. During the small hours of the morning he would leave his own premises and make his way to the matron's lodgings, returning in his pyjamas later in the night. Members of the sixth form who had not taken kindly to the new incumbent spotted his nightly forays and after one such enterprise obtained a pot of red paint and a pair of wellington boots. These they dipped in the paint, and when the Headmaster looked out of his window early that summer's morning he saw to his horror a trail of red footsteps leading from his front door to that of the matron's and returning to his home. Taking a rag soaked in paraffin, he hastily tried to mop up the footprints before his wife awoke, but unfortunately the sixth form boys took photographs which they sent to the Chairman of the Governors with some indication of the nightly habits of the Headmaster, who thereupon resigned. Getting to the top of the tree always involves hard work, but you have to be careful when swinging from one branch to another for the ground is a long way off!

The Headmistress of my own neighbouring girls' grammar school was the victim of an enterprising trio of ladies. Enid Godwin Of the Mary Datchelor Girls' School was in the habit of spending her holidays in Scotland in the summer and was usually away for several weeks. In South London in the inner city, many of the streets are made up of terraced houses with flat roofs, and it so happened that the premises next door to her home were vacant. This became known to a local entrepreneur who managed to gain illegal access to the empty property and onto the roof through the trapdoor. He then found it easy to gain entry to the Headmistress's house through her own roof trap and then to open her front door. On returning from her vacation Miss Godwin found the odd item of food in the pantry which she could not recall having purchased and some disarrangement of her clothes in the wardrobe. As she had arranged for her daily help to call in once or twice whilst she was away to water house plants, she did not take much notice of this. After one such summer vacation, however, she began to get telephone calls early in the term asking for appointments with ladies variously described as Rita, Tracy and Shirley. It soon became clear that her house had been used as a brothel during her absences.

Another such establishment was uncovered in one of several properties owned by my own governors where the lady in question was barely equipped with a bed, chair and cashbox when we evicted her. Fortunately, although the governors were my employers, neither they nor I were found to be living on immoral earnings. Neither was I able to enjoy the hospitality of the lady concerned, for as I related earlier our statutes in any event abjured me not to 'frequent ill houses'.

After a history of three and a half centuries it fell to my lot to make the first appointment of a mistress to the staff. In those unenlightened days no proper facilities were provided in the school for ladies and any woman who required the use of a lavatory had to use the Headmaster's. There was some spirited opposition in the common room, and a few of the more chauvinistic older housemasters subscribed to the view that:

> *The fat man with his steak and bottle*
> *Restores our faith in God Almighty*
> *But a woman reading Aristotle*
> *Destroys it all in Aphrodity.*

Nevertheless I appointed a young and nubile French mistress to engage the fortunate members of the sixth form in conversation. This was universally applauded by the boys, who were less dessicated than their mentors. Unfortunately early in the term, mademoiselle left the latch off the lavatory door, which I gather is often the practice in that foreign land where such facilities are shared by the sexes. So there she sat on the seat as I entered, clearly and audibly enjoying her mid morning stay over the watering hole.

'Je suis désolée, Monsieur Directeur!' she cried,

There are just a few moments in life when the *mot juste* comes readily to hand and all I was able to reply was 'Oui oui Mademoiselle.'

CHAPTER SIXTEEN

OUT OF THE CLASSROOM

The governors and the pedagogue
Were walking hand in hand
They wept like anything to see
Such fools about the land
'If they could see the light!'
They cried 'It would be grand'

'If all the sense in East and West
Formed one harmonious whole
And Buddhist monks replaced the cars
Which creep from pole to pole,
Who'd care for grubby profits then
If he could save his soul?

'Dear readers' smiled the pedagogue
'Our catalogue is done
Will you endorse our shining plans?'
But answer there came none -
And this was scarcely odd, because
They slumbered everyone.

Amongst those who labour behind the scenes in any well-ordered school are hard-working governors, bursars, secretaries, headmasters' wives and other ill-rewarded dogsbodies. In dealing with governing bodies it is as well to remember that there is nothing a man cannot achieve as long as he lets others take the credit for it. Nor is it any less true that behind every man there is a woman who could not be more surprised. There is an apocryphal story of a headmaster who was sick and was unable to attend the meeting of his Governors. His wife telephoned the clerk and the matter was brought to their attention at the meeting. At the end of the proceedings it was agreed that a motion should be sent on behalf of the board to the Headmaster wishing him a speedy recovery to good health, passed by nine votes to eight with three abstentions.

Governors come in all shapes and sizes, and many may well be old boys of the school. Looking round at my own body gubernatorial I could not help thinking of a few lines which Dr Allington, then Headmaster of Eton College, quoted extempore at an old boys' dinner.

The hall of fame is very large
And it's also very full
Some get in by the door marked push
And others by the door marked pull.

Nevertheless the steady application of hard work also helped, and l was to have the help of some excellent men amongst them who started in very lowly circumstances as boys at the school, some later to become millionaires. One of my better-known old boys, Michael Caine, in his days as a scholarship boy at 'the prestigious Grammar School' is described as finding himself 'as out of place as a rusty hubcap on a Rolls Royce'. He was not apparently much enamoured of alma mater. He recounted how my predecessor left many marks on his backside.

Most of the old boys who became governors were men of wisdom and good sense, but from time to time we had one who thought he knew everything, which was very irritating for those of us who did. One such member of the committee was Chaplain to Her Majesty the Queen in the Tower of London, where he was appropriately confined. His name was John Nicholls. During his incumbency, which he held in plurality with the living of St Mary Woolnough in the city, he was also Chaplain to the Lord Mayor of London and took his customary part in the Lord Mayor's Show. The carriage moved slowly round the city streets watched by the crowds on the pavements whilst John and the Lord Mayor acknowledged their applause. After some time John, who was not a young man, felt the call of nature very strongly in the form of acute pressure on the bladder. Unable at last to contain himself, he told the Lord Mayor that he would have to ask for the procession to halt at the next public convenience or he would have to give way to a most unfortunate release.

'Don't worry, my boy' said the Lord Mayor. 'Just move over this way.' He then lifted the seat, which concealed a commode and John sat down again, surreptitiously directing the flow with one hand while waving to the crowd and the television cameras with the other. His activities at the Tower of London included the redecoration of the Chapel of St Peter ad Vicula, in which is to be found the tomb of Queen Ann Boleyn. At an early stage in the work he was overcome by a manic curiosity, and when a suitable moment arose he lifted the lid of her coffin. The skull was indeed, as the song suggests, tucked underneath her arm and the remains of the Queen were plainly identifiable, with the extra finger she was known to have showing clearly on one hand.

Nicholls was well connected. Visitors to whom he introduced me included the Queen Mother and on another occasion King Hussein of Jordan, who was an old friend of his. He told numerous unpublishable stories of various sojourns he had enjoyed at royal palaces. His contacts at the palace enabled him to obtain the services of the State Trumpeters of the Household Cavalry for a memorable 350th anniversary on Founder's Day. Dr Matthews, then Dean of St Paul's (an old boy of the school) was there, the Bishop of London took part, together with the Lord Mayor, and the second lesson was read by Sir Alan Cobham (another old boy) who made the pioneer return flight to Australia in 1926. With over a thousand in the congregation and many other dignitaries present, the Headmaster read the first lesson, but unfortunately omitted to turn to the New Testament for the next reader. Sir Alan shortly after went to the lectern to read and, finding the bible open at the wrong page, had no recollection of the chapter and verse to which he should turn. And so he stood and stood, and a great silence fell upon the assembled multitude. The time passed. Minutes elapsed. Eventually the vicar moved across from the choir, turned to the lesson and read it.

A recording had been made of the service to be sold to the school at Christmas and Nicholls and I went to town to hear the unedited tape. There came the moment when Sir Alan was to read his passage. We timed the hiatus at about four minutes. During the silence the great man, who had done such valiant things for aviation, was heard to say 'Jesus Christ help me' The Queen's Chaplain said 'That is the most heartfelt prayer I have ever heard uttered in a church'.

Nicholls was something of a maverick. One Sunday he had agreed to preach at a church in Edinburgh. Arriving late to find the service already started, he suddenly realised that the hymn which was being sung was the penultimate one before the sermon. He thereupon bounded up into the pulpit and before an astonished incumbent could say him nay delivered his address. It was only after he had disrobed in the vestry that he found he had been preaching in the wrong church and was unknown to the vicar.

Like many headmasters it was it was my privilege on speech days and at other times to entertain a galaxy of the good and great. Lord Carr (then home secretary), Sam Silkin (Attorney General), Baroness Young (Leader in the Lords and my tutor's daughter), Sir Gerald Templar (the former CIGS) and Sir William Penney, who produced the British hydrogen bomb. Penney told the story of Professor Urey's lecture tour of America when he spoke to audiences at a number of university campuses. After several such addresses, becoming bored with giving the same talk at each stop, he suggested to his driver, a man of some intelligence, that perhaps next time he might take his place and read the script for him. To his surprise the chauffeur agreed, and with the latter's cap in hand Urey sat at the back of the hall at the next stop whilst the driver took the stage and gave the talk. After the applause, and pleading the pressing of time, he rapidly gathered up his notes and began to leave the platform. Unfortunately, however, a man jumped up and said he was the senior physics master at a high school and could the speaker just answer one very brief question before he left because he was uncertain about a small point of detail he had mentioned concerning the relationship between two of the uranium isotopes. Without hesitation came the reply 'I am surprised that any physicist would not be familiar with that matter. Why even my chauffeur on the back row could give you the answer.'

Up stood Urey, chauffeur's cap in hand, to confound an appreciative audience as the real chauffeur speedily left the platform and hurried out of the hall.

Other visitors included Dean Matthews of St Paul's (an old boy), Lord Hill of Luton (the most entertaining speaker I have ever heard), Sir Frederick Ogilvy (onetime Director General of the BBC), John Christie and Sir John Habbakuk, all three Principals of my own college at Oxford, and more recently the Speaker of the House of Commons, Bernard Weatherill. Weatherill recounted how at a dinner he had recently attended for Commonwealth speakers of parliament at the University of Saskatchewan he had been introduced by the Vice Chancellor as the Member of Parliament for Great Britain. On touring the school he was delighted to find that the prefects still wore gowns and that due ceremony was observed on public occasions and at morning prayers. 'The importance of ceremony' said the Speaker over our lunch, 'cannot be overemphasised. Dress and long-established custom reflect not the man but the dignity and gravitas of the office which he confirms and enhances.' There had been many young teachers in the difficult years of the seventies on my staff when the generation of the graduates of the sixties entered our schools and colleges. 'Do away with gowns!' they cried. 'Let the children call the staff by their Christian names, let us all dress in jeans and sandals. Away with school uniforms. Let us all put on the raiment of equality.' Those headmasters among my colleagues who resisted these siren calls earned the thanks and support of the great majority of parents. I was never ashamed to be called an educational coelacanth in these matters by a public school headmaster friend.

The Speaker went on to talk of the importance he attached to the modes of address which are traditionally used in the Mother of Parliaments. When he calls upon the Right Honourable Member for Midtown to speak, this confers a dignity upon his office as a member, representing his own constituents. Devoid of that dignity of dress and address, how much worse was an occasion in the Australian House when a former Speaker shouted to a member 'Sit down, you bitch!'

It is probable that there are those of the generation of the sixties who confused the dignity of ceremony with snobbery, of which there was, at one time, an undoubted excess in the Groves of Academe, together with the class structure of English society, which in spite of John Major's inaugural prime ministerial pledge remains with us today. As for myself, bankruptcy for my father during my infancy, a tough village school, an unemployed parent throughout the thirties, to be followed later by rescue through the grammar school, Oxford through scholarships, an army commission in the war and to field rank after on the Territorial general list, public schoolmastering and Headmastership provided an opportunity to bridge the whole width of class division, as they did for many others.

It works both ways. Members of Militant infiltrated a certain teachers' association which I attended as a guest. Unaware of my own difficulties in those early days when my mother had to pawn her wedding ring at Christmas time, they made it clear that they regarded me as one who had been fed with the silver spoon. After a few drinks, angered at some taunting, I treated them to a few details of those early struggles, of the sequestering of some of our furniture and life on the dole in the thirties. There came the response spoken from the heart 'Why didn't you tell us before?' It seemed that they had claimed me as one of their own. But I felt as remote from their world as I did from that of an officer with whom I shared a tent as a young captain in the 8th Army. He was one of the less attractive alumni of Eton, a school from which I have since met some delightful people. He had been commissioned into a rather more fashionable regiment than myself. His monosyllabic response to overtures of friendship during the first few days of our acquaintance were transformed into acceptance only when he found that we had mutual friends among his more able school fellows who I had known at Oxford.

There is much to be said for the steep climb uphill rather than the gentle coast down. The steep and rugged pathway is the better road and the temptation with the silver spoon is to dip it yet again and again into the honeypot. I had sat at various times at table with four Prime Ministers, Wilson, Thatcher, Heath and Macmillan. Three had climbed the rugged pathway up which I had taken my own far fewer faltering steps. Wilson, in his earlier days in the Principal's lodge at Jesus with Mary, his wife, had dazzled with sparkling wit, whilst Heath at a Royal Geographical Society dinner delivered the most lacklustre after-dinner speech I have ever suffered. Thatcher, when for a time I chaired the Headmasters and Mistresses of the Voluntary Aided Schools, was the Headmistress of us all, whilst Macmillan, across the table at an Oxford Society dinner talked to me behind those hooded eyes of the days when we had both been in the Mediterranean in 1944.

From those days I treasure a letter in his own hand from Field Marshal Montgomery. His deputy, Brian Horrocks, called his biography 'A Full Life'. Those for whom the cup of life is full and flows over can indeed count themselves fortunate.

CHAPTER SEVENTEEN

FULL CIRCLE

For now as life's long labour brings reward
And you into the sunshine turn your face
The purpose and the pleasure matched at last
The burden passed to others in the race
Walk now with joy along the woodland ways
And let the healing balm of nature spread
Its benison which sweetly soothes the soul
For now it is the primrose path you tread.

'The best club in the world' said my Chairman when I announced my intention to retire, 'is the one you are about to join'. For everyone there is an ambivalence of feeling about the onset of the occupational menopause. At times there is a temptation to regard work as an interruption in one's social life. At other times one is inclined to the view of Sir Norman Birkett, the great advocate, who in his biography wrote:

'I think that men and women who choose their job and find a pleasure in doing it are fortune's favourites. That a happy home life is the greatest of human blessings. That there is infinite wisdom in the old words 'Whatsoever thy hand findeth to do, do it with thy might'. That it is wise to have a hobby of some kind and if it is a useful hobby so much the better; that you should take every kind of trouble to keep friendships in repair, particularly as you grow older; that excess in all things is to be avoided; that it is wise to keep one's word, not to break promises; that a sense of public duty should be cultivated, if only as a safeguard against selfishness; that it is wise to keep the mind alert by reading and by all agencies such as TV and radio that now exert themselves for our benefit. I think is wise to realise the value of a margin in all things and not only in money matters, and not to spend too much time in seeking mere pleasure; and not to live for the moment only. In the end it is life that teaches all.'

Life does indeed teach all. And some of the most important lessons are those we learn when we are very young. Robert Folghum, quoted recently at a Royal Society of Arts Lecture, said: 'All I really know about how to live and what to do and how to be I learned in kindergarten. Wisdom was not at the top of the graduate school mountain, but there in the sandpit at Sunday school. These are the things I learned: share everything, play fair, put things back where you find them, clean up your own mess, don't take things that are not yours, say you're sorry when you hurt somebody, wash your hands before you eat... live a balanced life... stick together... goldfish and hamsters and white mice and hamsters all die, and so do we.'

Even so, as Maurice Chevalier said, I prefer old age to the alternative.

A few years ago I went back to Jesus College Oxford, where, along with the surviving freshmen of my year half a century ago and their wives, we were royally entertained. I was asked to propose the toast of the ladies, and as this reflects in lighter

vein in verse much of what has gone before I quote my few
lines of doggerel from the Jesus College Record:

Before I thank the ladies for all that they have done
I commend their great good fortune in the class of '41
For some wines soon need drinking and are early past their best
And others lose their potency or never pass the test
But the Jesus College vintage château-bottled '41
Encapsulates perfection, for its class defers to none.

Alight full 50 years ago with post-pubescent fires
Up from the Principality or sunny English shires
Meyrick scholars* from their hayricks, bucolic boys from Wales
Coal dust in their turn-ups and beneath their fingernails
Leavened by the English, left their Celtic country home
For the groves of academe and the philosophy of Rome.

There were those who worked their socks off to become respected doctors
And others soon submerged beneath gate fines and deans and proctors
Pursued by Percy Seymore** or unfortunate collections***
With heavy bills for battels and untimely predilections
For ladies lurking in the lanes or worse at Parsons Pleasure
Until donnish disapproval was soon to get their measure.

For the ladies up at LMH wore stockings. that were blue
And those who saw the tops of them were far between and few
And 'tho we thought we had on offer something no one could refuse
They wouldn't submit at Somerville or yield to us at Hugh's
And so for sublimation we played games or drank our ales
For those were days when they could still play rugby down in Wales.

In 46 returning to the body academic
Substituting martial forays for disputation and polemic
We next sought lifetime sinecure in college cures of souls
Whilst others found salvation in more money-grubbing roles
With perks from Unilever, Marks and Sparks or ICI
Preferring dining out with Mammon to pie up in the sky.

For there were those who went and did while those who couldn't do
Departed for didactic jobs where assets don't accrue
Becoming dons or schoolmasters or similar humble creatures
And those who couldn't even teach endeavoured to teach
teachers
Whilst others sought a richer but a less demanding fare
Living amid the fleshpots in a professorial chair.

So in our Celtic twilight or darkling English dusk
We gather here for dinner attired in deep subfusc
To celebrate survival of 50 glorious years
Surrounded by good company of undergraduate peers
Each one of whom has weathered less well than we have done
But who all give thanks to Jesus, floreat collegeum!

*Scholarship closed to Welsh candidates.
**Seymore was Junior Dean responsible for discipline.
***Collections :An internal college examination.

Old men reminisce and try to come to terms with their own experience of life and make some sense of it. At the age of 90, as I play out extra time in lighter vein, I am reminded of James Naylor's few lines:

189

King David and King Solomon led merry merry lives
With many many lady friends and many many wives
But when old age came over them with many many qualms
King Solomon wrote the Proverbs and King David wrote the Psalms.

Then again, as the shadows lengthen and in more sombre vein, I succumb to the temptation to end with a few more lines of my own verse:

I have been there before
Whilst reality slept in the womb of tomorrow
Which is today, the passing picture show
Flickering out its last few frames
Before the reinstatement of the void
What I have known I will no longer know
Yet here attends no fear or sorrow
But just a closing of the door.

I have been there before
Oblivious of the yesterdays of time
Through an eternity that sparks into this present light
Whilst all around the galaxies were born and died
Blossoming and then fading into blackest night
Unknowable behind an adamantine
And as yet unopened door.

I have been there before
And all who are today were there with me
We knew not nor did one from other know
Yet passed into this light of common day
In love and brotherhood until the stay
Was past and then the closing of the door.

We have been there before
Return we not alone to that unknown
Where present, past and future meet
And all creation coalesce where time is not
Whilst harmony supplants the entropy man fears
And all is one where none compete
Avowing they alone
Unlock or tend the door.

Have we been there before?
There is no need for man's consistory
Transcending all we know or cannot know
Confounding those who may presume

Tenure and sole enlightenment of truth
There yet remains above here and below
The enigma and the mystery
Behind the unopened door.

And so the door opened and closed too soon for so many of those we knew and loved in those days, now so long ago. In one sense, of course, they have lived on in our memories. RAF fighter pilots who sat beside us as schoolboys, university friends who joined the OTC with us and volunteered as soon as the time came for us to do so. Others of the 46th Infantry Division who never lived to meet annually with us for our feast of memory and remembrance. We that are left grow old and age wearies us.

The best left long ago. At the going down of the sun and in the morning we will remember them.

A LAST APPEAL TO REASON

BY

ADOLF HITLER

Speech before the Reichstag, 19th July, 1940

Hitler's Last Appeal To Reason, given to the Reichstag on July 19 1940

Beating the INVADER

A MESSAGE FROM THE PRIME MINISTER

IF invasion comes, everyone—young or old, men and women—will be eager to play their part worthily. By far the greater part of the country will not be immediately involved. Even along our coasts, the greater part will remain unaffected. But where the enemy lands, or tries to land, there will be the most violent fighting. Not only will there be the battles when the enemy tries to come ashore, but afterwards there will fall upon his lodgments very heavy British counter-attacks, and all the time the lodgments will be under the heaviest attack by British bombers. The fewer civilians or non-combatants in these areas, the better—apart from essential workers who must remain. So if you are advised by the authorities to leave the place where you live, it is your duty to go elsewhere when you are told to leave. When the attack begins, it will be too late to go ; and, unless you receive definite instructions to move, your duty then will be to stay where you are. You will have to get into the safest place you can find, and stay there until the battle is over. For all of you then the order and the duty will be : "STAND FIRM".

This also applies to people inland if any considerable number of parachutists or air-borne troops are landed in their neighbourhood. Above all, they must not cumber the roads. Like their fellow-countrymen on the coasts, they must "STAND FIRM". The Home Guard, supported by strong mobile columns wherever the enemy's numbers require it, will immediately come to grips with the invaders, and there is little doubt will soon destroy them.

Throughout the rest of the country where there is no fighting going on and no close cannon fire or rifle fire can be heard, everyone will govern his conduct by the second great order and duty, namely, "CARRY ON". It may easily be some weeks before the invader has been totally destroyed, that is to say, killed or captured to the last man who has landed on our shores. Meanwhile, all work must be continued to the utmost, and no time lost.

The following notes have been prepared to tell everyone in rather more detail what to do, and they should be carefully studied. Each man and woman should think out a clear plan of personal action in accordance with the general scheme.

Winston S. Churchill

STAND FIRM

1. What do I do if fighting breaks out in my neighbourhood?

Keep indoors or in your shelter until the battle is over. If you can have a trench ready in your garden or field, so much the better. You may want to use it for protection if your house is damaged. But if you are at work, or if you have special orders, carry on as long as possible and only take cover when danger approaches. If you are on your way to work, finish your journey if you can.

If you see an enemy tank, or a few enemy soldiers, do not assume that the enemy are in control of the area. What you have seen may be a party sent on in advance, or stragglers from the main body who can easily be rounded up.

Beating the Invader – a notice issued by the Ministry of Information with a message from Winston Churchill, Prime Minister

The Masters XV, Bedford Modern (NSF centre front row with ball)

Inspecting the Cadet Force, Bedford. From left: Headmaster, officers and the General

Dinner at Bedford Modern for staff who went on to become heads of
public schools or grammar schools

Headmaster, 1958

Rotary President, with Kathleen

Opening of new school at Sutton - left to right: Lady Jeans,
Col. W R Bowden, Lady Habbakuk, Kathleen Friskney, NJF and
Sir John Habbakuk (Vice Chancellor, Oxford)